Sex
What Your Parents Didn't Tell You

by
Michael Rittenhouse

© 2014 Vox Verbatim

Michael Rittenhouse

All rights reserved

www.michaelrittenhouse.com

Acknowledgements

Much of this book's content is based on Judeo-Christian teachings, which are essentially public domain. However, they are not common knowledge.

One individual in my life braved the cultural taboo on frank discussions of sexuality to bring those teachings to my (and others') attention. This inspired my first putting pixels on-screen, and his further encouragement ("This needs to come from the laity,") prompted me to seek the assistance and put forth the labor necessary to turn this book from a dream into a reality. Fr. Dwight Duncan: Thank you.

Many others have encouraged me along the way by hearing me out in those conversations by the firepit, once dinner has settled and the smoke and cognac have eased the fearless sharing of ideas and opinions. I prized those moments more than any of you may ever know. Thank you, my friends.

This book's marketing budget was crowdsourced. In fact, raising more than three times the intended amount was what finally, fully convinced my doubting heart that the book would be successful. While I would like to praise my supporters by name in front of everyone, they have not expressed a need to be so recognized. So, although I have said so in private many times, here it is for the public record: Thank you for making this possible.

Every work of art has a muse, of sorts. Mine is my family. It is my hope and prayer that my children (and theirs) can come of age in a culture that seamlessly reintegrates healthy sexuality with every aspect of life. Further, by sacrificing so much toward this book's creation, they have made the public purpose of this book into a personal one.

Finally, two public-school English teachers who probably never met each other helped me grow in my gift of writing: Mrs. Geneva Fulgham and Mrs. Donna Pecsenye. You overcame my hardheadedness with instruction and touched my spirit with your praise.

— Michael Rittenhouse

To my wife.

Contents

Preface 1
What I Saw at the Buffet 5
Masculine & Feminine, Male & Female 13
Orthosexuality 31
Liberators 51
American Prudes 69
Natural Law 81
Higher Goods, Lower Goods 93
Masturbation & Porn 99
Talking to Your Children 115
Epilogue 133

1
Preface

I began writing this book after asking many of my friends this question: Did your parents talk to you about sex?

The answer came back "No," almost across-the-board. So I wasn't the only one who had to learn by trial-and-error.

I came of age in the time of disco, MTV, lap dances, and sex-by-the-third-date. Without much in the way of guidance from home, I bounced from one influence to another, never quite grasping what was right but learning all the wrongs the hard way.

I was fortunate in that I didn't father any children out of wedlock, or otherwise dole out damage that couldn't be undone. But others in my cohort weren't so lucky. Some can't seem to stay married. Others speak and act, with alarming frequency, as if they aren't. Many look at their kids and think, "What the hell do I have to teach them about sex and relationships?"

And all of us who weren't given a firm foundation in matters sexual could surely use one now as we try to live our own lives out … and equip our kids for a world that looks even more shaky than the one we grew up in.

For many, the answer is to seek a strong spirituality in the Judeo-Christian tradition. That can work, and I encourage it. But there are churches out there that do too little (or do it badly) to promote healthy sexuality among their members and to counter the destructive influences wrought by the culture. Further, the world has six days each week to undo whatever good we get on the Sabbath.

And many, many of us, whether inside or outside of churches, don't want to hear about sexuality from a clergyman. That's understandable, given the way media have trained us in "separation of church and sex."

I have looked around for books aimed at people like us. Some are obviously meant for people already in the Judeo-Christian camp. Their distinguishing characteristic is the metaphor comparing sexual relations to the relationship between Jesus and his church—metaphysically valid but ineffective with marginal or non-believers. Official church teachings on sex tend to have an authoritarian sound to them ("Do this, and don't do that, because that's just how things are."), so there remains a big gap between the church and adults accustomed to making their own decisions.

Meanwhile, on the secular side, there's a raft of books claiming to remedy this or that sexual shortcoming. I found few with much other than physical remedies for sexual problems—most of which turn out to be emotional and spiritual, not physical.

As a people well-educated in physics and industry, we tend to address malfunctions like an engineer: There's something wrong with the design (the clitoris is too high; the penis too sensitive) or with the staging (try scented candles or more lube). This approach unfortunately sells books by the thousands, and when their solutions don't really work, we tend to keep reading them because we're attracted to the promise of an easy fix.

So I've written this book not so much as a "how to," but as a "now what?" for a general audience, everyone from the well-schooled orthodox Christian to the completely unchurched. That's a broad reach, but I've learned that the basic principles of sexuality are the same for all people at all times:

- The best sex happens when you lose yourself in it, not when you try to control it.
- You reap what you sow.
- This isn't a contest.

Still, my purpose in writing isn't to tell you what to do. Neither is it to tell you what to think. It's to help you think for yourself, free from the influences of the clueless or those who simply want you to be like them—the self-serving know-it-alls who publish the same worthless sex advice year after year. I am confident that when you understand sex as nature intended it, you'll waste no more time chasing bad advice.

In trying to "get it" myself, I've made a lot of mistakes and learned from them, eventually. Many of the chapters ahead lead off with those experiences, so be prepared for some graphic accounts as I call in airstrikes on my own (former) positions. All the best literature teaches with images, sometimes real and sometimes legendary. I write best about what I know, which is the most useful advice anyone ever gave me about writing.

Having operated behind enemy lines, what I've learned is that our sexual nature isn't that complicated. The biology is complex and fascinating, from pheromones to zygotes to the immunities conferred to nursing infants. But that's useful mainly to the white-lab-coat people; to understand your own sexual metaphysics, you need simply pay attention to real life. When a Liberator (more on them later) tries to convince you that only a Ph.D can properly instruct you in the use of your sexual energies, he's probably making too much of too little. Or, he's trying to deceive you.

Sex is organic. Nature dictates what we do. Metaphysics tells us why. And once we understand how our upbringing, culture, and selfish human tendencies can disconnect us from our nature, we can see the way to a thrilling, fulfilling, fully integrated sexual life.

—Michael Rittenhouse

2
What I Saw at the Buffet

If anyone says that sex, in itself, is bad, Christianity contradicts him at once. But, of course, when people say, "Sex is nothing to be ashamed of," they may mean "The state into which the sexual instinct has now got is nothing to be ashamed of." If they mean that, I think they are wrong. I think it is everything to be ashamed of. There is nothing to be ashamed of in enjoying your food: There would be everything to be ashamed of if half the world made food the main interest of their lives and spent their time looking at pictures of food and dribbling and smacking their lips.

—C. S. Lewis

One day I watched a man try to kill himself, at lunch.

He looked about like you, or me, with a couple hundred more pounds to take along. He did so with obvious difficulty—leaning hard over to lever himself off his seat, staggering with each step, standing sideways to reach the buffet because his belly prevented a head-on approach.

I wondered how, over time, he'd allowed himself to reach this shape without grasping—or, perhaps, caring—how he got there.

In a small number of cases, obesity has a medical cause. But for most of us in the abundant North American-European civilization, an excess of body fat results from habit: Too much input, not enough output. The body stores unused energy in a way that—let's be honest—neither looks good nor feels good.

It happens faster than we'd like when we're surrounded by processed food that's more calorically dense than at any time or place in human history. Meanwhile, the demands on our bodies have slackened. A grown man's physique is capable of plowing a field with oxen, but when the biggest effort of his day is to open a pickle jar, his excess calories have nowhere to go but sideways.

Too much input, not enough output. We grow where we don't want to. But we continue, often resuming the same habits after a crash effort to right ourselves.

Isn't that also the pattern of a troubled sex life?

Picture, for a moment, an 18th Century plowman with his team of oxen. He would live his whole life never seeing YouPorn.com, or, for that matter, high-fructose corn syrup. Would we say he was deprived?

Nothing in his natural environment could artificially pump his appetites up beyond his own needs. Not even on a trip into town would he have to try to ignore a young woman jogging past in a sports bra, or a billboard hawking endless pasta and free breadsticks. (I've encountered both on the way to work.) All his food was organic and minimally processed.

As a boy, the plowman knew about sexual intercourse from the farm animals; mating was no mystery. As a young man, he learned spirituality from his father, with his priest for backup. Connecting with his (eventual) wife would come as naturally and clearly as the sunrise. The only "-sexual" he knew—Orthosexuality—would unify them for life.

I am not suggesting the plowman would be sinless; only that he didn't live in an environment that constantly badgered him to override his own nature and needs.

Physically, mentally, and genetically, we're born the same human beings as the plowman. But the influences around us run much more numerous and seductive.

With mass media, there's never been so much "sex" available. I put that in quotes because most of it isn't actual sex (as in sexual intercourse) but the trappings of sex: bare skin, innuendo, bedroom imagery. But it all points to real sex, and as advertising goes, it's everywhere. The Internet itself took off when marketers discovered they could sexually stimulate others anonymously, through chat rooms, direct messaging, and ultimately, cameras. The World Wide

Web, regarded as a basic utility now, can function as a "porn pipe" into everyone's house, and no matter what URL you're on, you're only two clicks away from a sex act. (We will look at the newly discovered effects of this in the Masturbation & Porn chapter.)

For young adults, especially those in college, there's a bubble of sexual liberty that may have had forerunners in history but was never facilitated by a 24-hour communications network. (At school, I always knew a kind of hookup culture existed in little pockets among the privileged—the frat houses were known for hit-and-run sex—but the vast middle class of young women at that time didn't show much interest. That's changed.[1]) The pressure to join in plays on an instinct that's quite real and persuasive. Dustin Hoffman nailed it from the male perspective when he told an interviewer that being a young man is like waking up every morning "chained to a maniac." For females, it's the pressure to catch and hold the attention of a marriage-worthy male.

Adding to the confusion is an army of marketers committed to thinking up new ways to push our appetites to the red line. They've convinced us that more is better in everything, from portion sizes to sex partners.[2] They throw messages in front of us everywhere we turn, designed to make us override our own defenses. Doubt that? Recall that for more than a decade, they convinced us we should drink eight glasses of water a day, whether we were thirsty or not. There was never any scientific support for that, but we did it anyway, because we heard it from every direction.

---

[1] "Sex on Campus: She Can Play That Game, Too," *New York Times*, July 12, 2013 http://tiny.cc/nytimescampussex
[2] Exception: pubic hair.

When we, the intended audience, are confronted by so much unhealthy influence, our answer shouldn't be the reactionary, "What would Grampa do?" (My grandparents would not have been prepared for the Internet.) Rather, it's "What would a sane, stable individual brought up on, and grounded in, natural law, do?"

Commonly, the overload of sexual stimuli causes many to react rather than respond—hookups, masturbation, and artificial birth control have become norms because we've let ourselves be convinced there's no alternative; we're "born that way," with appetites that cannot be managed, only accommodated. They also appeal to our general reluctance to admit the need for self-control. Note how many bestselling fitness books promise ways to slim down while eating "all you want." Neither does chastity sell; rather, it's a novelty to which we make an occasional, unserious nod.

Our weak attempts at convenient self-medication address only the symptoms, like a candy bar eaten in lieu of a meal. As we will see in later chapters, what's really needed is to understand, forgive ourselves our weaknesses, and right-size and tune our own input and output to bring them more in line with our nature.

We have a healthy, sexual appetite built into us. It's a physical and metaphysical good, and it leads to more goods, like eye-fluttering pleasure and the generation of the next generation. And like the food appetite, it can be driven up artificially by external forces as well as by disturbances in the psyche. Stimulating the sex appetite out of proportion to its nature changes how we treat others and ourselves. (This also applies to efforts to deny sexual energy, as we'll see in the American Prudes chapter.)

I keep returning to the grand analogy between sex and food because both appetites have a dual purpose, or end. Sex has both a unitive as well as a procreative end: It brings male and female emotionally closer, and it brings valuable, new little humans into existence. Likewise, eating is a pleasure we naturally want to share with loved ones. A Hindu proverb summarizes this as, "Food offered without affection is like food offered to the dead." Or, more recently, from Emeril: "It's a food of love thing."

But separating these dual purposes fractures the human spirit. Take the conviviality out of eating, and you have *Soylent Green*—room-temperature ration pellets for breakfast, lunch, and dinner. Or remove the physical benefits, and you've reverse-engineered bulimia.

In sex, discarding one of its two purposes similarly shakes up the psyche. Hookups impair one's ability to mate for life (as we'll see in Talking to Your Children), and surrogacy—bearing someone else's child for money—severs the crucial bond between mother and child.

There's also the matter of maturity. As we grow, we have new impulses to master. A baby doesn't need to manage his energy input (food) or output (exercise). But as he grows into an adult—especially in a food-abundant, labor-avoiding society—an imbalance can literally weigh on him unless he masters his energy flow. So it is with the sexual urge.

But the grand analogy has one shortcoming: the existence of male and female, of masculine and feminine, which have no such analog in nutrition. It takes both sexes to make healthy sex, and like trapeze artists swinging toward one another, a failure of one spoils the whole performance.

We would do well to look now at the differences between male and female, and what happens when those differences are glossed over, or ignored.

Sex: What Your Parents Didn't Tell You

3
Masculine & Feminine, Male & Female

Don't waste time pursuing the ideal woman. Instead, work on becoming the ideal man.

—Unknown

I met Klaudia as she rang up my groceries. I asked about her accent; she told me she was from Poland. So, this being the final months of the Cold War, on my next visit to the checkout I wore a red-and-white Solidarity button I'd received from an emigré. She laughed and told me to wear it often. Assured that she wasn't an apparatchik, I invited her to lunch.

Only as we took our table did I learn she was 18, a high-school exchange senior. Having just graduated from college, I suddenly had to decide whether our five-year age gap was a problem. But as lunch turned into an afternoon, she proved mature beyond her years, setting me straight on the distinctions between Milton Friedman and F.A. Hayek while challenging me on Adam Smith.

As we got to know each other over the next few weeks, Klaudia talked at length about the high-school politicking she said she dreaded, mostly rumors of sexual deviance and promiscuity among her U.S. classmates, some of it verified. She claimed to be a sideliner in these affairs, having been ostracized for letting slip to her host family about her classmates' bed-hopping on the senior trip. The story got back to the school administration, and Klaudia ended her final semester as an outcast.

She seemed ambivalent about the wrongness of her classmates' acts, as if she couldn't find a comfortable position between her host family's horror and her friends' decadence. Having left that world five years ago, I had little to offer, and absolutely no stake. Eventually, I learned to change the subject.

Meanwhile, our time was running out. After graduation, her student visa would expire. We had just a few weekends to see each other until then, and we made the most of them.

The next time we were alone, I pressed her for sex, as I had always done with women, and she put me off without explanation. I figured a girl that young didn't really have to explain herself, so I let it go. She felt nice enough just to be around.

On her last night in the States, Klaudia asked me to take her to dinner. Leaving the restaurant, she had me stop by a grocery store while she went in for a jar of Taster's Choice, apparently a prize behind the Iron Curtain. She had something else in the bag that she didn't show me. At my apartment, she revealed it.

Condoms. She had a plan, with me in a supporting role. I turned the lights out and scooped her up off the couch, carrying her into my bedroom, laughing. Then we got very quiet, and she let me undress her for the first time.

On returning from the bathroom, she announced it was time for her to go. I reluctantly pulled my clothes on and drove her home. We parted, lingeringly, on her host family's front porch, promising to stay in touch. The knocker made a dreadful, final clack as she closed the door.

I returned to my apartment as the sun rose, ready to sleep off my exhaustion. I stopped in the bathroom to brush my teeth, but the first sight of my own face in daylight gave me pause.

Bloodstains, everyplace in the bath and bedroom that Klaudia had touched. My horror eased when I concluded that an untimely menstrual cycle must have begun during our encounter. This would have to be our little secret, and I hoped she wouldn't be too embarrassed. Perhaps, eventually, she would laugh about it, as I did crawling back into bed that morning.

One week later, a letter arrived from Poland. She'd written it on the flight. But her words conveyed little warmth; only wistfulness for a moment having passed. Only then I realized that the evidence left in my apartment had originated not from her menses, but from her maidenhead: She had chosen me.

At last, all her high-school drama made sense. The pressure was on her to lose it by graduation, and she'd only missed deadline by a week.

A present-day high-school teacher told me the kids see their situation like this: All the girls are psychos and all the boys are con artists.

I remember that. We wanted the girls to be more like us, and less like a high-end computer with a failing hard drive that looks great on your desk but just won't boot.

But on those occasions when a girl really did behave more like we said we wanted—which is to say, like a guy, with her own, chained maniac interrupting her every thought—

I wasn't the only one who found it disconcerting. We couldn't get our adolescent heads around it then, but it's the sort of puzzle we touched on in those late-night phone conversations between friends, the calls that carried on until we fell asleep with the phone in bed.

For all our confusion over why girls seemed so difficult, no one told us the most elemental difference is rooted in, and analogous to, our differences in anatomy. We are male and female, hence masculine and feminine.

The male projects. He has something powerful outside of himself that needs control from within.

The female receives. She has something internal of great value. It needs protection by her, and, ultimately, by him.

In my stunted development, I didn't see this in what had happened between me and Klaudia. I only felt vaguely as if I'd taken something to which I wasn't entitled. As if I'd shoplifted accidentally, but couldn't return the goods. That she didn't tell me her plan ahead of time suggests she also knew there was something inherently wrong about her decision.

I felt awful for Klaudia, and, eventually, for all the other girls anxious to discard their sole physical manifestation of metaphysical purity.

Of course, it's exceedingly difficult for the others after one female in a social circle offers her body up to a high-value male. Easy sex is a bait that any competitor can set out to catch him.

Still, had I been better instructed as a young man, I might have served as the responsible party in our relationship[3]. But many males carry a little secret: We really don't know what we're doing.

My suburban cohort came of age in a time when our fathers were gone all day. Their work consisted mostly of meetings, phone calls, and paperwork—nothing they could teach us side-by-side, the way a carpenter, farmer, or merchant could. They had little use for physical strength or for the hunter's instincts. They earned a respectable living and made safe, comfortable homes for their families, but many seemed to lack either the time, knowledge, or will to educate their sons about masculinity. Perhaps they'd heard it was no longer important. Perhaps they were never taught about it themselves.

This was a time in which masculinity had fallen out of fashion, at least in part because of cultural confusion over what the word meant. Like chastity, it drew withering fire from the Liberators, whose academics dismissed gender itself as a "construct"—a strange conclusion, given that nouns in a quarter of the world's languages have masculine or feminine gender, and languages themselves are organic. The Hollywood culture, always focused on optics, couldn't portray masculine men except as subjects of exaggeration or ridicule (as we will see in the Liberators chapter). Clint Eastwood's famous line about "feeling lucky" had to be delivered with a cocked .44 Magnum in hand; real police resolve most conflicts without brandishing weapons.

---

[3] One reason a boy should be instructed in the manly manners—holding doors for women, for example—isn't just that these are "nice" practices (nor, as radical feminists posit, are they a means to put women down), but they introduce him, in a physical way, to the concept of masculine responsibility.

But a straight line runs between the failure of masculinity in my generation, and the degradation of femininity as it played out in my encounter with Klaudia. Without masculinity, femininity seems a waste of resources. (More on that below.) Genders, like the yin and yang in Taoist philosophy, complement each other to form a whole. Imbalance triggers failure of the whole. The two elements combine, rather than oppose.

To recognize masculinity's absence, first we should define it:

Masculinity is a gender, which is different from a sex. It describes the manner in which one relates to the world.

Do I project my will, or do I let it be shaped by others? When a situation needs a leader, do I move into that position of authority myself, assuming its responsibilities? In communicating, can I let my silence speak as effectively as my words?[4]

Masculinity's core element is self-mastery.

A famous boxer once said that the fight was won not in the ring but in the weeks of training beforehand[5]. No competitor stood nearby to rally his workouts; neither did an audience. The focus and strength had to come from within the fighter himself.

---

[4] The Kipling poem "If" (http://tiny.cc/kiplingif) lists these and a good number of other masculine qualities. They're more complex than summarized here (a subordinate can be masculine as well as a leader, for example), so please see the Epilogue for more resources.

[5] Muhammad Ali, who is unfortunately known as much for his bluster as for his dedication.

Masculinity cannot be obtained from, nor supplied to, others. It is solely the product of one's own well-disciplined mind and body.

Rounding out the definition with a contrast, **masculinity stands apart from its bastard nephew machismo, or macho.** We've all seen the male who preens, intimidates, and bullies. That's because macho's most important aspect is appearance. To succeed, *macho always requires an enabler.* If, for example, your pimped-out ride goes unnoticed in traffic, you've wasted much time and money. And if you don't have a wife, you can't be a wife-beater.

Macho often looks like a cartoon of masculine, drawn by someone lacking a proper model. It's no coincidence that the most ostentatious displays of machismo appear in the ghetto, where fathers are scarce and where the girls fall for it because it's all they've ever known. But macho pops up anywhere that fathers fail in their responsibility to rear confident, self-reliant sons.

Macho is to masculine as a thigh holster is to concealed-carry[6]. Macho succeeds by demonstration; masculine, by quiet discipline.

I first noticed my cohort's confusion over masculinity on the first day of high school, when our chorus teacher announced she would separate the class into the four vocal parts: soprano and alto for the girls, tenor and bass for the boys. Immediately all the 9th-grade boys announced they would sing bass—even though only half of them could actually hit the low notes. If any of us had ever been told that plenty of full-grown, masculine men sing tenor, we

---

[6] Concealed-carry is a burden as well as a privilege. A firearm worth packing is probably large enough to cause discomfort, and that discomfort must be borne in silence.

didn't let on. We just knew that deep voices were a man thing. The girls were watching, you know. We couldn't afford to be seen by them as tenors, lower classmen, nullities … eunuchs.

Young women in such environments can also find masculinity confusing, because they've been taught early to compete with boys for class placement, college admission, and ultimately, job offers, pay raises, and promotions. I've noticed that in the illustrated children's books published since about 1980, the first depiction of a police officer, construction worker, or mechanic will most likely be female. Advocacy groups continue to pressure traditionally male institutions such as the military to put women in roles for which they aren't physically suited. Most mainline churches have yielded to activist demands for female pastors. Despite these changes and others, a note of crisis is periodically raised about the difference in earnings between men and women. Girls are taught early and reminded often that they're at a perpetual disadvantage, and pressured not to let boys have anything to themselves.

Children get the message that the differences between male and female don't matter much. And that's often where their instruction stops, leaving them to silently choke down their cognitive dissonance or risk ridicule for questioning the official line.

Meanwhile, in my upbringing, the macho boys bullied the others.[7] Obsessed with their own standing and oblivious to self-discipline, this was all they could do with their inchoate male instincts to exercise power and dominance. Then, once puberty hit, for lack of a proper rite of passage into

---

[7] One reason most "anti-bullying" efforts will fail is, they can't address the cause: poor fathering.

manhood (typically a test of physical and mental endurance, such as mastery of a craft, or a traditional hunt), they turned to conquering their only other rivals—the girls.

The rest of us knew little other than to follow their lead.[8] After all, the Liberators had already taught us that we couldn't be men until we'd ejaculated inside a female. To complete the act of intercourse was our highest aspiration as teens.

And this is how girls get tricked into treating virginity like an outgrown pair of shoes. They've been taught all their lives to treat males as competitors. If the boys go all-out to lose their V-card, why shouldn't they join in?

In this case, the boys can't be counted on to stop them.

Despite the Liberators' efforts to stamp it out, masculinity keeps trying to make a comeback—a testament to its place in nature. The masculine dilemma found a voice in what was called the Men's Movement of the early 1990s, a reaction to the desperate state of a generation of young men who'd been taught that their redemption lay in sexual conquest—a hollow reward, as it turned out. But the phenomenon appealed only to men willing to admit they were missing

---

[8] We weren't all failures. It takes a moment to remember those boys who didn't make a scene everywhere they went; didn't bully their peers; kept generally quiet; and excelled (though unobtrusively) in academics and in extracurricular activities. Recalling them takes an effort, because they never drew attention to themselves. Even when teachers, coaches, and the like held them up for recognition, they modestly accepted their due, then stepped back out of the spotlight. Today, they hold positions of leadership. Also, they got (and kept) the girl. The bullies haven't fared so well.

something. Also, the Liberators piled on ridicule from every direction. With little cultural memory of what masculinity really meant, the movement foundered and a state of confusion persisted.

Then came the development of "game," in which men learn to present themselves in ways young women find hard to resist, with the goal being to have sex on liberated-male terms. Game included common-sense measures such as a confident attitude, good posture, dressing well, and always being seen in conversation—in contrast to the quiet guy that all the girls ignore.[9] While game encouraged assertiveness, the focus was on technique, not character. Too much strategizing—and not enough foundation—makes for little more than a game. Sadly, as game practitioners' own forums[10] make clear, women must be available as enablers, which tells us this is machismo science, not masculine. The message of game turned out to be just as fractured as the one of my directionless teenage cohort: You're not a man unless a woman lets you ejaculate inside her.

Also in the '90s, we heard much about "alpha males" from various Liberators, the idea that only men who project dominance will rise in the business, social, and mating worlds. Unfortunately most alpha behavior looked like what had been observed among primates, which is to say, a lot of posturing and threatening—again with the macho, and again, needing an enabler in the form of an approving audience. In the human world today, truly successful males look and act more like Bill Gates or George W. Bush. They get the money, the power, and the girl by quietly leading and

---

[9] Unfortunately, "game" easily turned into a con game, like feigning skills such as palm reading ("chick crack") to lure girls into letting you initiate that first, critical touch. See http://tiny.cc/congame.
[10] http://www.pick-up-artist-forum.com

serving the needs of others. In sum, alpha appears to be little more than ghetto machismo for college graduates.

Working separately but simultaneous to all this, at least one psychotherapist pointed to the heart of the masculine problem, the dichotomy between "doormat" and "jerk" in a culture that knew no middle ground. Dr. Jama Clark authored two editions of a fast-selling book, *What the Hell Do Women Really Want?*, based on research into "mating behaviors" and aimed at guys who wanted a mate, but couldn't figure out how to get one. In her Seattle-area practice she found many males playing the wimp, oblivious to the masculine qualities that would make them attractive. For starters, this meant taking the lead in dating and relationships. Two generations of Liberators' sensitivity training had left them puzzled over the eternal question: Why do girls always go for jerks?

The simple answer is that while jerks aren't desirable *per se*, they at least appear more masculine than the wimps.[11] Call this women's sound rejection of the market value of men who had apparently never learned masculinity from those in the best position to instruct them: their fathers.

(Assuming they grew up with one, in a nation where more than 40 percent of children are born out of wedlock.[12])

Lately, there's evidence that young men are simply checking out, eschewing the demands of masculinity and choosing instead to entertain themselves right out of circulation.[13]

---

[11] The writer George Gilder affirms the idea that true masculinity is a prized if misunderstood quality: "Men already know that if they are to win a high-status woman for more than a brief sexual fling, they had better gain high status themselves. There are few facts of life that men know so well."
[12] CDC data: http://tiny.cc/17vghx

We have a cultural problem, in that advanced societies tend to devalue the masculine qualities. (This lasts right up until those qualities are needed: Witness the widespread reverence for policemen and firemen in the days right after their heroic losses on September 11, 2001.) Women share the blame for this when they praise males who exhibit people-pleasing, essentially feminine traits such as emotionalism and compliance—the wimp side of the macho coin. This does not describe a male who leads and pioneers, though he's certainly easier for a woman to manage ... right through to the eventual divorce.

If the stalemate over masculinity and femininity is to be resolved, men will—per their nature—have to take the lead.

First, they have to learn to disregard the Liberators, who are well-entrenched and persuasive in entertainment, education, and public policy. The anti-masculine element of Liberator doctrine was set forth clearly in 1909 by a Progressive who succeeded both in academia as well as politics. While president of Princeton University, Woodrow Wilson said, "The purpose of a university should be to make a son as unlike his father as possible."[14] In the decades that followed, government would enact welfare policies that made husbands and fathers superfluous. These policies are now part of our historical narrative, suitable for teaching in schools as fact rather than theory.[15]

---

[13] See Dr. Helen Smith's *Men on Strike*, 2013.
[14] Wilson would affirm this belief in a 1912 presidential campaign speech. It persists today, as noted by author and commentator Dennis Prager: "Eighty-eight years later, the president of Dartmouth College, James O. Freedman, echoed Wilson: 'The purpose of a college education is to question your father's values,' he told the graduating seniors of Dartmouth College."

Next, there are the skeptical peers, a byproduct of Liberator sexual culture, who must not be validated. In my early 20s, I had a peer who showed me how to do this. He was blessed with many of the outward qualities women find hard to resist: six feet of height, quiet self-confidence, a well-developed physique, and a college degree. But he also had unusual spiritual and moral strength, and constantly turned away sexual advances from girls who, understandably, wanted to bag him. They knew sex was the surest way to get a guy's attention, and he knew it, too; what he also knew was that he didn't want a woman who bargained on those terms. His stiff-arming left them frustrated and often contemptuous. Even his friends couldn't resist whispering that he was a closet homosexual.

Today he's a family man, his marriage free of contamination by memories of second-rate sexual exploits. But in my life's experience, he was the exception; most of the men I knew in my 20s weren't anywhere near that well-disciplined, and the women around them played right into their weakness, which ultimately exposed their own.

What's also needed for young men are life activities that focus on the fact that manhood requires internal strength, continuous movement toward independence from others (including females), and spiritual growth. Worshipping beautiful women and, ultimately, one's own ability to conquer them, ends with everyone losing.

As with most false doctrines, liberation includes a fragment of truth. In this case, it's that humans need redemption. I'll elaborate on this in the Orthosexuality chapter, but in brief: While even first-rate sex can be deeply gratifying, it can't

---

[15] Dennis Prager, "Conservative Parents, Left-Wing Children," http://tiny.cc/Pragerquote

make us whole. Our error is in seeking redemption from a person—another, inherently flawed human.[16]

Breaking the stalemate requires women to be more like women, as well. "If a woman does not force him to make a long-term commitment—to marry—in general, he doesn't. It is maternity that requires commitment. His sex drive only demands conquest, driving him from body to body in an unsettling hunt for variety and excitement in which much of the thrill is in the chase itself."[17] Nobody wins at this game, although the media make a lot of money portraying sexual conquest as a symbol of manliness, and female imitation as "empowerment."

As noted in the Masturbation & Porn chapter, I'm seeing signs that young men are searching for a better life than the endless, ungratifying falsehoods preached by the Liberators. But they aren't getting the message soon enough in a culture that sexualizes everything.

The greatest revolution in history—the American Revolution—originated with family men who sacrificed their personal interests for the betterment of all. In other words, they manned up, and in so doing created a way of life that aligned with their nature to become the envy of the world. They rebelled against self-appointed leaders who tried to rob them of their natural rights.

---

[16] This theme runs through many popular love songs. Phrases like "can't live without you," "you're my everything," and "can't stop thinking about you" praise the redemptive power of another person.
[17] George Gilder, *Men & Marriage*, p. 47

Today we face a similar oppression of our nature from authorities whose crackpot notions of sexuality drive us all to confusion and destructive behavior.

Can we save it? I'm optimistic about the value of individual effort, because in my lifetime alone, I've seen the following "impossibles": grassroots women rose up to defeat the Equal Rights Amendment; the Berlin Wall came down; concealed-carry became the law of the land; violent crime plummeted; and political conservatives rallied to control the U.S. House of Representatives—twice. Opportunities to reverse Liberators' gains exist all around us, disguised, in the famous phrase, "in work clothes." Some of these opportunities appear too small to matter, but they appear precisely where Liberators have made their most damaging inroads: Little League teams and Boy Scout troops never have enough leaders; neither do Sunday-school classes.

Men's failure to step up lets a whole society fall. But it's not just our inherent laziness[18] at the heart of the problem. When we don't submit ourselves to a higher authority, we become the sole, flawed authority. Our human failures tend to make us dictators answering only to ourselves, causing the very "Daddy issues" that demoralize our children, corrupt relationships, and eventually spill out into the political arena. Then the Liberators show up with their deceptions to finish it all off.

Leadership comes with risks. For example, fathers who encourage their sons in spectator sports may unintentionally project their own machismo and try to live out their

---

[18] Men's chief sin is shirking responsibility, dating back before history. In Genesis 3, Adam ignores his wife such that she falls under the influence of an evil, spiritual power. Then, when called to account for his disobedience, Adam blames "The woman whom thou gavest to be with me."

fantasies at their boys' expense. The reality is that extremely few high-school ball players make a career in their chosen sport, and the demands of practice eat into limited academic and skills-learning time. These shortfalls can be masked by the excitement surrounding the games. (Again: Machismo requires an enabler. Nothing enables the show-off like the roar of a crowd.)

But I don't want to limit my fellow fathers' imagination. Once they have a firm understanding of masculinity, it should be easy to see what needs to be done in their own father-son relationships. Reform begins with the reformer.

A commercial culture—movies, games, televised sports—drains men of the time and willpower to step outside of the "packet of urges"[19] with which they begin life. We would do well to curtail, or never allow to start, the media-driven activities that prey on our sons' need for adventure, replacing them with homegrown adventures and with skills teaching in areas that require practice and self-discipline, and which carry their own rewards.

Women also have to relinquish the reins. Behind every demoralized young man there is usually an absent or indifferent father, as well as a mother who, rather than help the father fulfill his role, tried to take it on herself. Decades of liberation have preached that sex roles—genders—are interchangeable. If this were true, we should have seen the development of stronger families, higher-quality men, and satisfied women over the past 50 years. Where is that happening?

---

[19] J. Budziszewski, *On the Meaning of Sex*, p. 58

A female pop singer cried plaintively in the '90s, "Where have all the cowboys gone?" It's the top complaint from young women today: that men aren't "marriage ready." Of course they aren't. Half of them grow up without full-time fathering, and it's anyone's guess how many of the fathers in place understand and embrace their responsibility to guide their sons toward responsible, functioning manhood.

Ultimately, it will be up to men to solve this problem, first by becoming what every woman wants, instead of just wanting every becoming woman.

Then we all have to re-learn sex not as an animal conquest, but as a unifying act that takes both participants out of themselves and into a higher level of being.

4
Orthosexuality

Sexuality is the expression of life and the antithesis of death.

—Alexander Lowen

For your first date post-honeymoon, you flew to Santa Fe. You spent most of the day window-shopping to kill a few hours before that night's charity ball, to which you'd been given tickets you could never have afforded on your ground-floor salary.

You hadn't planned much about this trip, so when it came time to find a place to change clothes and, later, to sleep, you were reduced to pleading with one motel clerk after another, as most of the local rooms were booked up that night.

You finally found a place along the Interstate. It reeked of cigarette smoke and the door opened onto the roaring highway. It would have to do.

At the ball, your youthful figures stood out among the prosperous, married, older couples for whom this sort of soirée was routine. On the dance floor, her narrow waist felt magnificent in your hands in between the twirls you loved to send her out on. She smelled wonderful, too, more salty, earthy than you remember. This couldn't just be from perspiration; on her skin you picked up something sweet, like a hint of cedar. The only change you could think of was, she'd stopped taking the Pill a month ago.

Social decorum kept you from touching her as you wanted; you would have to hold off until you could be alone.

You fell onto the double bed and charged into sex with little more than a nod to foreplay. Sooner than you'd expected, your hips started to move on their own, as if they'd been hot-wired. She sensed it, and her body began its own countdown sequence. No words, no guessing, no hesitation; it ended explosively after just a few minutes, barely in time to break a sweat.

You collapsed next to her, your mind swimming in a narcotic haze; she remained at arm's length, awash in her own flood of endorphins. As your breathing slowed, you felt your foreskin roll slowly over your diminished glans, sealing her moisture in.

You awoke later, surprised that you hadn't interrupted your trance to ready up for sleep. In the bathroom mirror, she gave you a long, knowing look.

The next morning, you picked up her scent again, this time on your own skin. She was in you just as surely as you were in her. You had melded, become one flesh, and that felt like no other sensation on Earth because it reached into the core of you, took something, and left something else behind.

While movies, music, magazines, and TV have done much to glamorize the hookup, they've done little to convey in words (or pictures) what a sexuality befitting our human dignity looks like. Hollywood can't hold our attention that long. But it can create snapshots of how we'd like to imagine life could be. Most of them include sex on demand between perfect young bodies, with no unpleasant aftertaste or anything so messy as a lifelong commitment (with a few exceptions, to be resolved by the closing credits). This ideal rarely plays out off-screen. Life is just too complex for that.

To point this out would cast an advocate like me as the abominable "No" man. So, at the outset of this book I knew I'd have to do more than just point out the Liberators' errors. The writer Bryan Preston gives a succinct phrase for why advocates for moral sanity keep losing to the Liberators: "You cannot beat something with nothing."

In all my research, I found far too many advocates railing against this or that; few state clearly and explicitly what we are for.

I knew I'd need a word for that. In finding one, I had to discard many.

"Traditional" as in "traditional values" doesn't fit because much of the American tradition is mere prudery (see the American Prudes chapter). This is so widely known that the Liberators use a caricature to stigmatize the very idea of Judeo-Christian sexual mores: "Missionary position and only for the purpose of reproduction." It's clever satire. Unfortunately, it's also widely supposed to be true.

Any terms that suggest limits, such as "correct," "normal," "ethical," "proper." Again, they sound like prudery.

"Christian" unfortunately smacks of "traditional" with all the baggage the Liberators have lumped onto it. It also implies that non-Christians cannot know great sex, and that's simply untrue.

Although accurate, **"monogamous" sounds like "monotony,"** and it's been hijacked to include "serial monogamy," a rationalization for hooking up or shacking up. Also, monogamy doesn't guarantee good sex (though it is a metaphysical requirement).

"Organic" finished a close second, because sexuality should be organic, but the word has too many other uses.

Even "natural" can mean whatever we fancy. Which is too bad, because a kind of naturality is what we're made for.

I didn't coin the word "Orthosexuality," but since it's obscure, I'm co-opting it.

Ortho- is Greek for "straight, upright, correct, regular," making Orthosexuality the sexual relations that our bodies, minds, and hearts were made for. It's at the core of our being, though often obstructed by the hangups and artifices that we—in all our neuroses, second-guessing, and misguidance—have tacked onto the simple, beautiful act of intercourse.

Its criteria are simple and few:

The best sex can only happen when you lose yourself completely in it.

This shouldn't surprise us, but in a time when so many live separate from the natural world—isolated by concrete, climate controls, LED screens, and the distortions of a marketing-driven culture—we can be heavily influenced by unnatural forces playing on our self-serving nature. The ever-present enemy of all human potential is the self and its drive to control.

This is nothing new to people who serve as therapists. Dr. Alexander Lowen, a psychiatrist and author, noticed in the early 1960s a growing number of patients who, although they led active and sometimes adventurous sex lives free from social strictures, sought his New York practice for help with complex sexual dysfunctions, as well as utterly banal ones. He wrote of his experiences in a multitude of books.

Dr. Lowen found that many of his clients had come to regard sexual intercourse as a performance, nobly claiming to want to "please" their partners with exaggerated selflessness and acquired skills.[20] "To the ego, the body is an object to be understood, controlled, and used."[21] The layers of pretense added up from there. As a consequence, Dr. Lowen's patients suffered premature or delayed orgasm, impotence, flagging desire, and other maladies—despite having thrown off the cultural taboos they'd always seen as their obstacle.

Decades after Dr. Lowen published his findings, the same sexual dysfunctions persist in an even less inhibited people. The Liberators haven't succeeded in liberating us.

Today, for example, anyone can find online testimonials by men—especially young men—swearing to "make her cum first" as if their penis had a switch labeled DILDO MODE. It sounds gallant, so it appeals to a male's inner knight. The core misunderstanding is that a true sacrifice wouldn't require validation from another party.[22] "Make her cum first" is the attitude of a man lacking confidence in his own masculinity, perhaps because, like so many, he doesn't know what masculinity is. It's also dualistic, separating the lovers as if they'd each been assigned a job description. One

---

[20] Lowen, *Love and Orgasm*, p. 14
[21] Lowen, p. 63
[22] Gilder, p. 46: "When a man says that a woman is 'good in bed' he usually means 'responsive,' i.e., appreciative of *his* performance." (Emphasis in original.)

cannot simultaneously "lose" oneself while maintaining status as a separate entity.

Women can also fail in this manner, turning sex into a performance for the purpose of snagging a high-status man. You can gauge this idea's popularity on the supermarket magazine racks, where every other cover promises "Ten Ways to Drive Him Wild in Bed!" Although not every woman reads or even likes *Cosmopolitan*, it's fair to infer that the idea of sex-as-performance has infected the female half of society. *Somebody's* buying this stuff.

In truth, and despite our internalizing the noble principle that others' needs must come first, sexual satisfaction "is not something one can give another person. It depends upon the ability to surrender oneself fully to the sexual experience."[23,24] Every act of withholding, affectation, and artifice piled onto sexual intercourse obscures this critical element: the complete surrender of the self to the act.

If you've ever taken a bungee jump or witnessed one up close, you know that any effort by the jumper to stay in control—flailing at the air or grabbing the cord—spoils the thrill.

---

[23] Lowen, *Love and Orgasm*. Further: "[Satisfaction] escapes the person whose sexual activity is a performance. No man can satisfy a woman or give her an orgasm. He can create the conditions that make possible her self-fulfillment, but the rest is up to her. The primary conditions are that he be fully himself, honest in his relationship to the woman, and capable of enjoying sexual contact with her."

[24] I quote Dr. Lowen's book extensively in this chapter, so he deserves a little introduction. Lowen was a practitioner of bioenergetics, the belief that emotional disturbances manifest themselves in muscle tension exhibited in various parts of the body. Like most pioneering therapists, he hit on many valuable insights. His understanding of healthy sexuality and disorders lines up very closely with natural law, as noted in the Epilogue.

Likewise, a life-affirming, mutual, orgasmic buildup and release cannot occur when one of the partners tries to stay in control. "Satisfaction results from the full surrender of the self to the partner in the sexual embrace.... [O]nly when lovemaking is wholehearted, or ... the heart is joined to the genitals in the act of sex, is it possible to attain orgastic fulfillment in sexual love."[25]

The beginning of this surrender is sexual attraction, which draws us out of ourselves to connect with another. We can quantify this to some extent, through study of the chemicals oxytocin and vasopressin, which cause emotional bonding between female and male, respectively.[26] But the laboratory merely affirms what one author discovered while writing the bestseller *How to Make Love to a Woman*: What humans (and especially women) really want is "a return to romance, a return to wooing and courtship, a return to traditional sex roles and the warmth these can bring."[27] Treating intercourse as an act of chivalry simply substitutes one form of chauvinism for another.

Orthosexuality avoids this zero-sum game of exchanging gratifications, combining two wills and bodies in a synergistic act that adds up to more than either could achieve independently. Expressed as a formula, Orthosexuality is 1+1=3.

Intercourse is defined by its two ends: unity and procreation. Or, you reap what you sow.

In a "How to Pick Up Girls" culture, it may sound revolutionary to point out that our sexual nature is defined

---

[25] Lowen, p. 38
[26] Dr. Joe S. McIlhaney, Jr., and Dr. Freda McKissic Bush, *Hooked*, Kindle location 652
[27] Michael Morgenstern, interviewed in *People*, August 9, 1982

not by its beginning (conquest), but by its end—procreation.[28] Actually, that's a natural-law principle, and it's true of any of life's activities. We only go to an airport because we want to travel to another place; the check-in counter is simply where we start. So it is with sex. The end defines the means; unity and procreation define sexual intercourse.

Unity is more than just a warm feeling of closeness. It's the exchange of something intimate, intangible, and permanent. "[I]f we try to eliminate this connectedness from sex, we remove the uniquely human aspect of it, and the sexual act becomes nothing more than raw animal behavior. However, when this connectedness is allowed to mature in the context of a lifelong committed relationship, sex is a wonderful, sustaining expression of love."[29]

But there's another qualifier. Emotional unity through sexual contact makes sense only in conjunction with sexuality's other logical end: procreation. Again, it's in the etymology: *pro-* tells us we are approximating something; *-creation* is new life. It's the way we're made. It's also how every one of us *was* made, in a heterosexual, genital union.

This doesn't mean every act of intercourse must result in conception. Nature frames human sexuality with a fertility cycle that leaves about 22 days per month for unity alone.[30] So the procreative act doesn't require intent to conceive, just an absence of preventive measures. This surrender embraces—or, in Lowen's term, expresses—life.

Couples who regularly open themselves to the procreative experience have described the moment of orgasm as a

---

[28] Budziszewski, p. 64
[29] McIlhaney and Bush, location 726
[30] I think of this as God's little reward for us being close and secure with one another.

transcendent glimpse of immortality. As with the bungee jump, relinquishing control unleashes the power of the experience, and procreation gives us a power unavailable through any other means. Through sex, we can bring into existence another living, breathing person. Call it spiritual math, again: $1+1=3$.[31]

The temptation for us selfish humans is to harness this power and channel it toward our own ends. Therein lies our downfall in sex, as in so much else. "The spiritual side of life can be separated from the physical only at the risk of destroying the unity and integrity of the whole being."[32] (Note that this essentially Roman Catholic statement originated from a secular Jew. Orthosexuality knows no denomination.)

And there's that word again, unity. When I hear of college administrators doling out condoms to students, I'm dismayed to imagine so many young lovers enjoying only a partial download of the sexual experience nature has made for them. Safe sex—conducted from opposite sides of a latex film—not only prevents disease; it prevents the surrender and union that make the sexual act transcendent.

To young people with sex lives characterized by masturbation, even condom-obstructed sex can feel like a step up. Unfortunately, it's a step on a surreal staircase that ends, Escher-like, at a wall.

Male and female are complementary, not competitors.

---

[31] Possibly this is why the Liberators, many of whom profess agnosticism or atheism, regard sex as their greatest religious experience. Having denied an actual God, they focus on sex for spiritual fulfillment.
[32] Lowen, p. 28

A growing body of research affirms the chemistry behind sexual unity. Once coupled physically, male and female trade secretions like two elements combining into a wholly new compound. His semen, absorbed through her vaginal walls, brings her a sense of calm[33]; her estrogen, taken up through an abundance of receptors on his penis[34], conditions his heart. The connection also opens internal chemical changes that reorient the mind:

> With sexual intercourse and orgasm, the woman's brain is flooded with oxytocin, causing her to desire this same kind of contact again and again with this man she has bonded to, producing even stronger bonding.[35]

Once she has opened her body to him, their connection grows from magnetic to molecular. She finds him difficult to leave. He returns to her even as he senses the temptation toward others.

An emotionally healthy man engaged in regular, procreative sex can testify how it changes his personality. Within minutes of his climax, he feels different all over, and it affects how he thinks, walks, and moves, for days.

> The neurochemical responsible for the male brain response and synaptic change is called vasopressin…. Often referred to as the "monogamy molecule," vasopressin seems to be the primary cause of men attaching to women

---

[33] "Semen Eases Depression in Women," State University New York at Albany. http://tiny.cc/womendepression
[34] The male's foreskin is supplied with estrogen receptors. R. Hausmann et al., "The Forensic Value of the Immunohistochemical Detection of Estrogen Receptors in Vaginal Epithelium," International Journal of Legal Medicine 109 (1996): 10-30.
[35] McIlhaney and Bush, location 402

> with whom they have close and intimate physical contact.[36]
>
> One long-term result of the mature love relationship that stays intact (and there are many such positive results, such as providing a stable home environment for child security) is a relaxed, trusting, loving, rewarding, faithful, sexual relationship.[37]

It may be needless to say, but Orthosexuality is limited to monogamous relationships intended to last a lifetime. In other words, to matrimony.

In a culture that no longer looks down on sex outside of marriage, single males may feel they're living a kind of pre-sentencing release, free to live it up before turning themselves in for a life term without parole.

But their behavior suggests they're already serving hard time. Single men:

- have one-fifth the sexual activity of married men
- commit nearly 90 percent of major and violent crimes
- have almost double the mortality rate of married men (and three times the rate of single women) from all causes.

Meanwhile, married men:

---

[36] McIlhaney and Bush, location 457
[37] McIlhaney and Bush, location 638

- are significantly less likely to be committed for mental illness
- are 30 percent more likely to be employed than single men
- earn 70 percent more than singles of either sex.

The writer George Gilder wasn't the first to collect these statistics, but he summarizes the transformation of males thusly:

> [W]ithout a durable relationship with a woman, a man's sexual life is a series of brief and temporary exchanges, impelled by a desire to affirm his most rudimentary masculinity. But with love, sex becomes refined by selectivity, and other dimensions of personality are engaged and developed. The man himself is refined, and his sexuality becomes not a mere impulse but a commitment in society, possibly to be fulfilled in the birth of specific children legally and recognizably his. His sex life then can be conceived and experienced as having specific long-term importance like a woman's.[38]

The crude expression, "You just need to get laid," has a ring of truth to it. But that would define our sexual nature by its beginning, rather than its end.

The pop psychologist Dr. Ruth Westheimer made a meme of the phrase "good sex." She left a lot of room for interpretation. But she also seemed to be driving at a reorientation of where an anchorless society—and the people comprising it—were headed during her time. What's the end of all this? Simply getting laid cannot be both the means and the end.

---

[38] Gilder, p. 14

For a man, an unmistakable sign of Orthosexual connection in the sex act—or, in Dr. Lowen's term, orgastic buildup—is a growing uncertainty of where his body ends and hers begins. This can terrify him the first time he senses it, and even in subsequent encounters, for the fear that his erection is failing.

Even an uptight male gets a glimpse of this opening-up just before orgasm. He starts to feel as if he's not fully in control of his body.

What's actually happening is, in being given over completely, his penis has changed from a projection to a bridge. A certain amount of letting-go is required for this, and it cannot be faked. It is also impossible through masturbation, beginning and ending, as masturbation does, within the same body.

If a man's been trying to control the outcome of sex at this point, he really ought to quit. "The process of excitation continues through the act of coitus itself until the involuntary movements of discharge occur."[39]

> Orgasm commences with the contraction of the bulbocavernosi in the man and in the woman. These muscles surround the base of the penis in the man and the introitus (opening) of the vagina in the woman. The orgasm is experienced as the opening of a dam, with the release downward of a flood of feeling while the body convulses as a unit in response to each involuntary forward swing of the pelvis. Feelings of melting and streaming downward now

---

[39] Lowen, p. 180

pervade the whole body. If the acme is intense enough, the sensation of heat increases and is perceived as a glow in the pelvis and as an overall body sensation of lumination.[40]

In the woman, the counterpart of ejaculation is the contraction of the smooth musculature surrounding the vagina. This action is perceived by the man as a "pumping" of the penis. Thus there are two involuntary responses in the woman that combine to give her the experience of a total orgasm: the convulsive reaction of the whole body, similar to the man's, and the rhythmic contraction of the muscles surrounding the vagina and in the pelvic floor. If the woman reaches her climax at the same time as the man, both responses are intensified.[41]

That's the physics. Here's the metaphysics, again from Lowen:

Precisely because religious communion can move us (in the emotional sense), we experience it as a valid expression of our link with the universe or God. Sexual orgasm is a deeper, more biological experience of man's unity with nature and the universe.

Glow and lumination are other aspects of this phenomenon that bear some resemblance to cosmic events. The full orgasm is generally accompanied by a feeling of glow that is a "higher," perhaps hotter, stage of the phenomenon of sexual heat. If the intensity and extent of the orgasm reach a high peak, the glow may extend over the whole body and be experienced as a feeling of lumination. The external manifestation of this feeling of

---

[40] Lowen, p. 196
[41] Lowen, p. 197

> lumination is seen as a radiance that is the natural expression of a person in love. Glow and lumination are properties of heavenly bodies. The person in love feels that he is in heaven. In love, the individual transcends the experience of his finite existence; in orgasm, he transcends the feeling of his physical existence.[42]

Or, in concrete terms: 1+1=3.

With all the cultural and personal baggage we carry from the misinformation we've absorbed, Orthosexuality is probably the exception and not the rule for many. A male who's masturbated from puberty into adulthood will have difficulty admitting a woman to his sensory loop.[43] A female who has either learned to use sex as a bargaining tool or to regard it as inherently negative or evil, can't easily connect her heart with her own genitals for the full experience of surrender.

Orthosexuality can happen only when we aren't trying for something else. It's the ungilded lily; the organic fruit. The perfection that is achieved not when nothing more can be added, but when nothing more can be taken away.[44]

This is where so many of the self-help sex books of the last 40 years have fallen short. They're focused on technique: how and when to touch here and not there; what sort of additions or flourishes can lead to the Big O. The contrast reminds me of the difference between Dale Carnegie's *How to Win Friends and Influence People* and Stephen Covey's *7 Habits of Highly Effective People*. The former is concerned with little more than situational tips and tricks; the latter

---

[42] Lowen, p. 204
[43] See more on this in the Masturbation & Porn chapter.
[44] Paraphrased from a quote by historian L.J.K. Setright

with reorienting one's thoughts to understand and accommodate the needs of others.

How have we gotten so bunged up about something as simple as sex? Lowen faults modern civilization's compulsive, deadline-driven lives for the excessive self-control blocking our sexual connectivity. He finds clarity observing the natural movement of a native woman untouched by schedules, benchmarks, and notions of productivity:

> I have said that in orgasm, one reverts to the kind of movement that lay at the origin of one's being....
>
> When one watches a West Indian woman walk, for example, one is aware of the ease and freedom of her movements. Her hips sway loosely, her legs move effortlessly, while the upper half of the body rides gracefully upon this carriage. [She] feels no compulsion to arrive anywhere on time. Most people in our culture move compulsively.
>
> What strikes us most about the walk of the West Indian woman is its sexual quality. It is sexual not because it is sexually provocative, but because it looks alive, vital, animal-like. It is sexual because the woman is conscious of her body, conscious of her movements, and identifies with the sexual nature of her being.

Forty years after Dr. Lowen wrote that, researchers would confirm that a "discerning observer may infer women's experience of vaginal orgasm from a gait that comprises fluidity, energy, sensuality, freedom, and absence of both flaccid and locked muscles."[45]

Possibly at some point in human history everyone knew Orthosexuality, just as everyone ate organic food and lived by the movement of the sun. Then came the controllers, and then the Liberators to free us from them, and the commercial interests looking to marketize whatever causes our glands to secrete the stuff that makes us want to buy things.

Even those fortunate ones among us who get sex right don't necessarily feel compelled to talk about it. For all they know, everybody else is having the same experience. Sex being a naturally private act, we don't share experiences with others the way we would about an especially good steakhouse.

Of course, not every orgasm brings that transcendent glimpse of immortality. Some of us rarely reach that height, held down by hang-ups, inhibitions, or false bargains pressed onto us in our upbringing. Even if one emerges from childhood and adolescence relatively well-grounded, the Liberators lie in wait to confuse us by deconstructing sex as if it needed a step-by-step instruction manual. Liberators haven't succeeded in improving our sex lives because they keep trying to add stuff when most of us need to throw stuff away.

Orthosexual sacrifice releases one's strengths by exposing one's weaknesses. By giving oneself entirely over to the act, one is no longer concerned with foreplay tick-boxes or with jockeying for position in some orgasm-olympic relay race. Gratification just happens.

---

[45] "A Woman's History of Vaginal Orgasm is Discernible from Her Walk," PubMed, Sep. 2008. http://tiny.cc/herwalk

Orthosexuality

Can we return to this? Maybe. The human tendency is to stay put, for the same reason a toddler will sit in a soiled diaper: "It's warm, and it's mine." When we find tolerable comfort, we usually stay with it, so we don't risk loss. Even as adults, we hold onto fallen investments, lousy lovers, and crummy jobs. With sex, perhaps we've come to believe that what we have is as good as it gets.

Orthosexuality is what remains after giving up all the self-serving nonessentials—even when they're disguised as serving others; about giving oneself completely and freely, not in a *quid pro quo*, but a total surrender of the will.

There's a close parallel to this in the social world. It's the romantic tradition of the ballroom dance.

Whether it's the swing, the waltz, or the two-step, what's most important is that the partners are touching and in sync. They know where to go, what to do next. This connection allows them to enjoy the moment as one. They even look like one, because functionally, they are.

The man leads. He chooses the steps, but only in a sequence that she can follow. And the woman follows; she finds his lead natural, comforting, and protective. It has to be, because he's leading her in directions she cannot see.

If either one withholds, the dance fails. So it is with the sexual encounter.

But if they relinquish their own wills, the pair can combine for an all-too-brief moment of glory demonstrating the beauty of human procreation: two complementary and opposite sexes united in forming a third, one greater than themselves, an immortality. 1+1=3.

Life.

It's the closest we will ever get to knowing how it feels to be God.

5
Liberators

Believe those who are seeking truth. Doubt those who find it.

—Andre Gide

I met Elaine in my second year at college. A robust, wide-shouldered blonde, she'd played competitive volleyball in high school, and watching her crouch below the net convinced me that with quads like hers, she could probably change a tire without a jack.

Off the court, her anatomically correct hips flowed into a snug pair of jeans in a way that spoke one word to me: Ready.

She liked athletic guys, which I was not, so she surprised me taking my invitation to join me at my apartment one night to watch a ball game. She matched me beer-for-beer, wisecrack-for-wisecrack, just like the Playboy *centerfolds said they did on weekends. We ended up wrestling on the floor, then through the door of my bedroom, where I could scarcely believe my good fortune when she reached to undo my belt.*

Finally. All my years of teenage frustrations, and many months of wandering this huge campus trying hard not to gape too hard at its bumper crop of exquisite young women, I was looking at the sexual exploit to end all, nothing between me and Elaine but a condom.

That layer of latex would be my undoing. I couldn't feel enough through it to build toward a climax. She sensed this after a time and invited me to go at her bareback, but even then my frustration, fatigue, and embarrassment made finishing impossible. My body wasn't the only part of me not responding; my mind also wanted to leave the room. I had felt something for Elaine, but right then I could feel nothing. Only much later would I realize why.

My heart wasn't in it.

Eventually I gave up, we traded awkward platitudes, and Elaine went home.

Months later, one year out from graduation and plotting my post-college life, I landed an internship on the West Coast. It happened to be in Elaine's hometown, where she was taking the summer off. I invited her out to dinner at a small Italian restaurant. She admitted she'd been hard to reach, because she'd been in the hospital. I asked why.

"You have to do something when you're four months pregnant."

She continued describing the complications of her abortion, but I barely heard her. I was mentally counting back the weeks since our cursed encounter. I knew it could have been mine because pre-ejaculate can carry sperm cells. Although my eyes had locked on the checkerboard tablecloth before me, all I could picture was a baby with my face, covered in blood.

But the timeframe didn't match; it couldn't have been from our encounter. Sensing my confusion, she admitted she wasn't sure who the father was, having been on a sexual bender that year mainly to get back at her own father, whom I'd briefly met when picking her up and whose dourness seemed to fit the dismal picture of home life she was painting for me now.[46]

> *I resumed breathing, and she kept talking. She needed to make her confession. I needed a much stronger drink than the chianti our waiter had set between us.*[47]

Once I'd recovered from Elaine's revelation, I was left with a mixed sense of relief and failure. At its beginning, our hookup looked like what our culture had taught me was the ultimate goal: a willing young beauty, a place to ourselves, and no social, religious, or family strictures to impede us. Not even the buzzkill of a "meaningful relationship" to get in the way of our autonomy. We could have sport sex, like the college kids on *MTV Spring Break*. At the end of it, I expected to feel as if I'd just won a medal.

Instead, I felt hollow. I'd chased an oasis right into a mirage.

This wasn't the first time I would be disappointed, nor the last. But I would keep trying in the belief that if I could just get the formula right I'd be living out the promises made in the pages of *Penthouse Forum*. Recreational sex was, after all, new territory in the human experience, or so my generation had been told. I might have to work a little harder to get my piece of it, and to get it right.

Thus continued the "progressive darkening"[48] of my soul, my willful commitment to an ideal whose origins I did not yet grasp.

---

[46] Years later she would call herself a bisexual.

[47] At that moment I reluctantly remembered one of my favorite quotes in literature: "The world and all our powers in it are more awful and beautiful than we can imagine until some accident reminds us."
—G.K. Chesterton

[48] A phrase from Pope John Paul II's *Evangelum Vitae* (Section 21).

The Liberators began to go public with their message of sexual freedom in the 1950s. Their enemy was a prevalent, suffocating social prudery that made even clinical discussions of sex uncomfortable, if not forbidden. In this, they had a legitimate case to make. Their answer, however, turned out to be just as demeaning to the human spirit.

Liberation ideology had its roots in early 20th Century socialism, which was itself heavily influenced by Darwinism's belief that humans were merely sophisticated animals whose behavioral edges could be rounded off with a bit of eugenics and/or social engineering. For their ideal—especially in sexual matters—Liberators looked to the primate world, specifically to the unusual habits of the bonobo chimp.

Bonobos are lauded for being "female-centered and egalitarian," a species that "substitutes sex for aggression. Whereas in most other species sexual behavior is a fairly distinct category, in the bonobo it is part and parcel of social relations—and not just between males and females. Bonobos engage in sex in virtually every partner combination"[49] including homosexual acts, and intercourse between mature chimps and juveniles. (I first noted the affinity for bonobos in nature shows, which cited all this in approving tones.)[50]

This appears to be the universal ideal for Liberators in all times and places: a social structure of sexual libertinism,

---

[49] Bonobo Sex and Society, *Scientific American*, March 1995. http://tiny.cc/bonobosociety
[50] For more on the bonobo-human ideal, see this Power Line blog post: http://tiny.cc/powerbonobos.

absent any natural law, and especially lacking self-discipline. In that sense, Liberator sex looks like a pie-eating contest: vulgar, yes, but it takes a strong man to turn down free pie.

Understanding that the human mind has no defense against images, Liberators began using photography and motion pictures to promote animal-based ideals, which would otherwise have sounded too dissonant to thinking people. Further, as the success of advertising showed, the repetition of even a wrongheaded message can make it stick.[51] The ability to put fantastic visions into people's heads used to be reserved for God alone. Now that power was available to anyone who could muster the funds for a camera and microphone.

For me—and everyone's experience was different— exposure to Liberator messages began with television. Our TV set made the perfect babysitter. In my pre-school days, our console-mounted RCA functioned as a kind of all-weather fireplace, with me and my sisters huddled around its glow until bedtime. In my schooldays, I came home and sat on the floor soaking up cartoons and reruns for hours at a time.

As the 1970s rolled along, prime-time programming took a turn away from the innocence of *Gilligan's Island*. Liberators, most famously the producer Norman Lear, put forth sitcoms brimming with caustic jabs at American culture. Naturally, these weren't meant to inform but to persuade, so the script writers caricatured their targets at every turn. Husbands and fathers took their lumps on *Maude*, *The Jeffersons*, *Soap*, and *All in the Family*. And we learned that

---

[51] "We grew up founding our dreams on the infinite promise of American advertising. I still believe that one can learn to play the piano by mail and that mud will give you a perfect complexion." — Zelda Fitzgerald

dads weren't even needed from *The Partridge Family*, *One Day at a Time*, and *Alice*.

Themes ranged from sexual roles and mores to economics to everyone's favorite scapegoat, racism. Ultimately the goal was to tear down notions of authority, replacing it with autonomy no matter how weakly founded. As for opposition, the prevailing parental-cultural establishment would have no say except to ridicule itself through caricatures and easy set-ups for punch lines. Pretty much anything associated with the past was ripe for a takedown, including, most prominently, traditional sexuality.

Of course, there were exceptions, notably family-oriented shows like *The Waltons*. But even I remember the father character rebuking organized religion in one episode, and John Boy turning the tables on a cartoonish capitalist. Dramas like *Family* and *Life Goes On* worked pro-homosexual propaganda into their otherwise family-oriented storylines. (These are standard-issue today, ushered along by *Will & Grace*, *Modern Family*, and *Glee*.)

Sex and sexual relations took front-and-center, because that's what the audience hungered for. My education began with *Love, American Style*, a prerecorded, sketch-comedy program spliced with wordless vignettes. My conscious memories of the show include a little boy playing the son of nudists who repeated the line (to adults), "I didn't recognize you with your clothes on," and a vignette of a man at his girlfriend's knees, struggling to open a bottle of champagne. As the cork popped, the camera cut to her startled, "Ooh!" face. Even as a child, I got that.

Then *Saturday Night Live* rolled out. Not in prime time, of course, but who wanted to be left out of the competition when all the other schoolkids were recounting the best and bluest lines on Monday morning?

These were my conscious memories of television, and my unconscious mind got the message, too. By puberty, I understood that sex was an utterly nonserious matter and was available to any male who persisted. There were no rules anymore. Any ideas about propriety belonged to the past. We, the Pepsi Generation, could say and do whatever we wanted, make our own decisions about right and wrong, and leave the fuddy-duddies spluttering in our wake.

As the biggest medium with the broadest reach, TV got most of the Liberators' attention,[52] but their influence ranged throughout the entertainment industry.

George Carlin and Richard Pryor were a couple of the biggest acts in '70s comedy. They fostered Eddie Murphy, Sam Kinison, Andrew "Dice" Clay, Martin Lawrence,[53] and others whose stage routines couldn't run more than a few seconds without circling back to bodily functions. They could be funny. They just didn't distinguish between genuine and embarrassed laughter. The latter requires less work and talent, but more profanity.

---

[52] See Ben Shapiro's book *Primetime Propaganda: The True Hollywood Story of How the Left Took Over Your TV* for a detailed account of the Liberators' takeover of Hollywood.
[53] Interestingly, all four comedians drew protest from Liberators over their content, which various Liberator constituent groups (feminists, homosexuals) deemed offensive. This contradicted Liberators' reverence for the comic whose prosecution for obscenity helped to open the age of off-color comedy—Lenny Bruce.

The movies—does anyone remember when ratings weren't necessary? Hollywood pandered to prurient and bloodthirsty appetites to such depth that MPAA developed a ratings system to defuse parental (and ultimately Congressional) protest. Not long after, cable television started piping skin, gore, and profanity directly into homes right past all but the most cautious parents.

Pop music iced the broadcast-media cake. Novelty hits like "Telephone Man" and "Push, Push, in the Bush" had us preteens snickering by the radio. In dance tunes, the word "love" served mostly as a euphemism for intercourse, as lyricists tried to write around community standards.[54] Eventually, MTV removed all mystery by turning the words into visuals, which by the rap era had begun to dumb even vulgarity downward.[55]

Meanwhile, the publishing business opened paths into the explicit. For the Baby Boom, this began with a bestseller called *Everything You Ever Wanted to Know about Sex but Were Afraid to Ask*. Its follow-up included full-page watercolors of naked people coupling, and fantastic portrayals of group sex. By the early '80s, Nancy Friday's sexual-fantasy collections were making the rounds at my high school. These read like *Penthouse Forum* letters. We drank in detailed accounts of incest, sado-masochism, and gender swapping for the same reason drivers gawk at car wrecks—the more graphic and taboo, the more captivating. These lurid sexual tales (none of which were true), captured our teenage imagination and affirmed that, just as we suspected, the whole adult world really was all about sex—and the adults in charge were keeping it from us.

---

[54] I had no idea the phrase "rock and roll" originated as a lower-class Southern euphemism for sex until I took a college course in pop music.
[55] Not all music was explicit or implicit about sex, of course. Innocent love songs continue to chart today.

At least two equally explicit best-sellers followed, purporting to instruct eager minds on the mysteries of sexual intercourse. *How to Make Love to a Man* and its mirror, *How to Make Love to a Woman*, topped the charts in 1982. Bookstores added new sections to hold all the copycats.

On the one hand, such writings fed our natural, adolescent hunger for explicit information. On the other, most of it was fiction, or speculation. But the written word's greatest power is its ability to cause the reader to gin up his own mental images—in this case, images that might never have occurred to uncorrupted people.

In the end, sex education for me and my generation consisted of unrealistic sexuality, presented as both entertainment and clinical knowledge. From people who knew better, such as our parents and the church, we heard … nothing. No debate can be won by a party who isn't invited, or who fails to show up.

———————

Mass media can persuade a whole culture to affirm or accept lies as well as truths because, again, *the human mind has no defense against images*. Efforts continue today on all fronts, simply because visual propaganda works.

To confirm this, we need only look at the example of the recent global-warming scare. With predictions of ecological disaster beyond human remedy, climate-change theorists inspired books, movies, in-depth news reporting, and a documentary-style film (*An Inconvenient Truth*) that reached schoolchildren as well as paying audiences worldwide.

(Global warming hitched a ride on '70s-vintage, Liberator-inspired scares about overpopulation. Long since debunked in fact, they retained enough cultural resonance to bolster the "guilt" aspect of global-warming theory.)

The movement's symbol took shape as a widely distributed photo of polar bears allegedly stranded on an Arctic ice floe, representing nature imperiled by man's carelessness. This touching image spurred a copycat picture published in a respected science journal. Both pictures later turned out to have been falsely characterized,[56] the latter an outright fabrication.[57] Data didn't support the alarmists[58], in any event.

But the momentum was on. Governments ordered "carbon trading" schemes to discourage use of organic energy. Corporations donned halos to crown themselves environmental saints replete with "green" PR campaigns. Homemakers paused before starting their dishwashers, unsure which time of day would be best to help stave off coastal flooding.

In the time since warming theories proved false and the campaign began to crack up[59], the public's perception has eroded only gradually. Many still wonder about those polar bears … because the human mind has no defense against images. (This is why everyone must take responsibility for what he sees, and what he allows his children to see.)

The Liberators know that on controversial topics, humans tend to believe the first side they hear. That's why political

---

[56] "Polarganda," a blog post by Tim Blair. http://tiny.cc/polarganda
[57] "Ursus Bogus," Tim Blair. http://tiny.cc/ursusbogus
[58] "The Settled Science of Polar Bears," Power Line blog. http://tiny.cc/settledsci
[59] As of this writing, with "global warming" looking unlikely, alarmists are shifting to the phrase "climate change" to encompass all types of variances.

spats over textbooks get so heated. Everybody, especially those peddling confusion, wants to reach the kids first.

The sum of all this persuasion at so many levels is a narrative. Narratives guide how we process new information.

Those raised on the biblical narrative see their world through the stories presented in the Bible:

> The world is a battleground of good vs. evil, with rewards waiting as the result of self-sacrificial acts, and punishment arranged for those who act purely in self-interest.
>
> Humans are born sinful and should always try to sin less, even though they will never reach perfection.
>
> Personal gain comes from serving others' needs first (a.k.a. free-market entrepreneurship) and taking risks.
>
> Resources and potential are limitless; all that keeps us from growth and prosperity is limited thinking and the desire to control others.
>
> Freedom is found not in self-gratification, but in self-control.
>
> Poverty is the natural state of mankind, and relative poverty is typically the result of chronic, poor decisionmaking by those living in relative poverty.

> Lord Acton's famous phrase, "Power tends to corrupt, and absolute power corrupts absolutely," means that government should be kept small and its powers decentralized and divided.

The Liberator narrative is postmodern. In this view:

> Religion was created by man to explain the unexplained; now that science has explained and solved so many problems (plagues, storms, famines), we no longer need to believe in a supreme, unseen being.
>
> Sin is a concept used by the ruling classes to keep the lower classes in line.
>
> There is no evidence of an afterlife, so life's goal should be to maximize personal pleasure and minimize sacrifice.
>
> A loving God would not punish people for following their nature.
>
> Injury, death, pain, and suffering happen at random. So does good fortune.
>
> You should be able to do whatever you want as long as you don't hurt someone else.
>
> Much of human behavior can be explained by observing animals, so humans probably evolved from animals.
>
> Income disparity can be remedied through social services and progressive income taxes.
>
> The rights and privileges of majorities should be sacrificed to accommodate minorities.

> Resources are limited, and humans tend to overuse them. We consume too much.
>
> Human nature can be perfected with the implementation of laws and policies designed to root out undesirable behaviors. This requires an ever-expanding government to administer.
>
> Good intentions matter more than results.

Late 20th and 21st century media operate within the postmodern narrative.[60] Most of the points listed above are reinforced directly or indirectly through the content in news accounts and popular entertainment.

Of course, the Internet now provides the bulk of mass media, and no one owns it. There is no Hays Code, no minimum age, no community standards, and no rating system. The only limit on what anyone can transmit or receive is bandwidth. You may think you've seen the worst of it, but you haven't. A week later, someone will upload a new low. That's our scenery now.[61]

In practical terms, it means one kid with a wi-fi enabled device can receive—and share with his friends—more than any brick-and-mortar porn emporium could deliver. The Liberators have been filling this pipeline for two decades,

---

[60] The best portrayal of the post-Christian ideal plays throughout the *Star Trek* series of TV shows and movies. Star Fleet personnel live in a cashless, socialist economy; religions are usually depicted as part of primitive or deeply flawed civilizations; in the end, human science and engineering always save the day.

[61] The Internet can also teach us much about humans' need for confession, repentance, and redemption. Any number of sites allow users to log on anonymously and post their deepest secrets. The downside of this is that in connecting with other like-minded individuals who refuse counsel, we can settle for validation rather than healing.

and the effects are just getting documented. (See the Masturbation & Porn chapter.)

Aside from pornography, the Liberators also use the Web to specifically target teens and children with sexual miseducation that, unfortunately, many parents still don't do much to insure against. Filling the void is a new breed of "sex columnist."

A few well-meaning advisor-types cropped up in the '70s, treading carefully so they could be syndicated in newspapers. But the Web opened the floodgates to a crudity that newsprint, delivered to doorsteps, couldn't handle.

The first novelty act appeared in a Seattle arts-and-entertainment weekly, in the form of a homosexual purporting to advise heterosexuals and homosexuals alike. (That's become a pervasive, bonobo-inspired Liberator talking point: There are no value differences among sex acts.) Other weeklies, seeing how the Seattle column could support their own advertiser base of strip clubs, escorts, and phone-sex lines, signed up for syndication. In short order, and with no qualification for being called a "sexpert," imitators popped up nationwide in college newspapers, most of which had already pioneered online distribution. Currently, there are too many such advisors to count, and they're happy to post their counsel for anyone to see—regardless of age.

Liberator sex advice is amazingly easy to write, as it all sounds alike. With orgasm taking the place of God, and with the bonobo chimp as the behavioral model, a Liberator's answer to every question becomes simply: If everyone involved in a sex act is of age, gives consent, and uses condoms, all is well. Those who disagree, including spouses, are disregarded as "sex negative."

All along, Liberators have repeated the same metaphysical blunder: They believe that individuals can get redemption from other people. But Liberators also share a fundamental error with the Prudes, against whom they claim to rebel: They both believe sex is a purely human activity, and God has no place in it.

What both sides lack is humility. They have all the answers and no interest in debate. Consequently, the Prudes, through silence, end up feeding their young innocents to the Liberators, whom the Liberators indoctrinate and spit out, accepting no responsibility for a culture plagued with self-indulgent males, confused females, and, ultimately, a self-perpetuating, single-parent tradition.

Today, a kind of multiple-meta-irony, we can see the previous generation's failure portrayed on *Mad Men*, where the '60s-era mother Betty Draper uses a go-to refrain whenever her children begin to vex her: "Go watch TV." Irresponsible? Yes, and of course we all act irresponsibly from time to time. I don't think my parents grasped what TV was teaching me. They had a pretty good moral compass, good enough for them to know to pull the cable when they caught me peeping at late-night softcore. But that temptation to delegate at least some of the care for one's offspring runs strong.

As a child, I had only the parts with which to build my own moral compass, and I can see now that the distorting magnet of TV programming would warp my ability to navigate the human landscape.

Now, the LED monitor—from palm-sized mobiles to wall-filling flat-screens—continues to deliver young people over to an entrancing world of ideas made overpowering through staged visuals. Video games feature anatomically unlikely, explicit physiques (male as well as female); webcams give exhibitionists a worldwide audience; porn portrays every woman as a sexual do-monkey.

Maturity can help us outgrow these influences. But that may not occur until well after adolescence and young adulthood, segments of life when we have the most opportunity to treat ourselves and each other badly. Even as adults, many of us are afraid to completely let go of Liberator culture because the Liberators convinced us there was no other alternative to the Prudes.

Another part of Liberator conditioning was the idea that we could not be hurt by what we viewed. Yet, can't we acknowledge that we all were, and continue to be, shaped by what we see on a screen? What man doesn't leave an action movie ready to level an imaginary gun at a bad guy? What woman can watch a romantic comedy without half-expecting to meet a handsome, witty young man poised to sweep her off, laughing, to the good life? The human mind has no defense against images.

A wise saying begins, "Watch your thoughts, they become words. Watch your words, they become actions…." Through careful self-examination, we can begin to understand how the Liberators deceived us when we were most vulnerable. By discerning what's good for us, we can take control of our input. Ultimately, this enlightens us to the power we have over our output.[62]

---

[62] Mark 7:20-23 "What comes out of a man is what defiles a man. For from within, out of the heart of man, come evil thoughts, fornication,

But the Liberators are only half our problem.

theft, murder, adultery, coveting, wickedness, deceit, licentiousness, envy, slander, pride, foolishness. All these evil things come from within, and they defile a man." Liberator culture panders to, and in many cases, reinforces our worst desires.

6
American Prudes

If [man] cannot accept his animal nature as part of his biological heritage, he will struggle with guilt and shame about his sexual function.... The spiritual side of life can be separated from the physical only at the risk of destroying the unity and integrity of the whole being.

—Alexander Lowen

> *On a plane ride one weekend, when Southwest Airlines still had "lounge" seating, I watched a family of six fill one lounge all by itself.*
>
> *After takeoff, I noticed them leaning all over one another, reading books together, feeding one another snacks, occasionally blessing each other with an affectionate touch or kiss.*
>
> *Their casual affinity and comfort made it look as if they'd all grown up together, even the parents. Here I had a glimpse of what life in their house was like, with everyone openly and physically acknowledging their dependence on each other for everything.*
>
> *And I wondered why, even with eight of us living in a three-bedroom house, my family was never that close.*

Queen Victoria made her reputation as an inorganic being when she reportedly admonished her niece not to breast-feed her newborn because "you are not a cow."

Regardless of whether that quote is apocryphal, the monarch wouldn't have been the first to regard human sexual nature as less-than-human. Centuries earlier, the philosopher Maimonides took aim at the penis itself, "to bring about a decrease in sexual intercourse and a weakening of the organ in question, so that this activity be diminished and the organ be in as quiet a state as possible."[63] The Gnostics didn't much like the body's appetites, either, and sought to distance themselves from biology in the belief

---

[63] *Guide of the Perplexed*, University of Chicago Press, p. 609

they could become more holy. Any number of Eastern philosophies follow a similar, ascetic model.

To deny or starve the carnal desires—be they for sex, red meat[64], or earthly thrills—elevates oneself, in this view. Only commoners and other unthinking people would let their urges run loose.

Mistakenly and commonly called Puritans or Victorians, the American Prudes see sexuality as something just a little beneath human dignity. Today they're dismissed as "sex negative," and the Liberators claim prudery is the only alternative to their own no-holds-barred sexuality. But it's never been that simple.

In America, there has been a long-running scrimmage between the Prude culture, which is mostly northern European and English in origin, and the earthy Mediterranean culture rooted in southern and eastern Europe.

These two cultures fight for influence in public policy, voting, and public opinion, and not just about sex. The pitched battles in law usually shape up over the vices. For example, guess which culture is the Mediterranean, and which is the Prude: In New Orleans, one can order, and consume, cocktails at a sidewalk bar at any time of day; but in Indiana, no one can buy refrigerated beer at a convenience store, or any beer at all from such a store on Sunday.

This doesn't mean that Mediterranean cultures are indifferent to vice. Rather, in a community where everyone

---

[64] In Latin-derived languages, the word "carnal" is closely related to the words for flesh, blood, meat, and sexual relations.

is known to be a penitent, there's less of a drive to control one another with laws that nobody really wants to enforce. Instead, the community—not the hard-edged, procedurally bound state—takes primary responsibility for looking after its members.

But if you really want to know whether an individual grew up in the Mediterranean or Prude culture, listen to him swear. In the heavily Catholic Mediterranean culture, anger is most commonly expressed in spiritual terms: *goddam this* and *to hell with that*. In Prude culture, it's the bodily functions: *screw this* and, in refined language, *take this invitation go to mate with yourself, or with your mother*.

People in Mediterranean cultures tend to view the body as fully integrated with the spirit. They're more open to affectionate touch, even between men.[65] Further, everyone's treated like family when under the same roof. I used to say I liked Protestant weddings and Catholic receptions, because the former only last a few minutes and the latter go on all night. We're all here, so let's enjoy each other as long as we can. (Full disclosure: I wasn't reared in a Mediterranean culture, but I could see one from my house.[66])

I am not arguing that Protestants are inferior to Catholics. Queen Victoria's influence touches everyone in America, and it's part of our general reticence over sex talk. This isn't

---

[65] James Lileks, March 21, 2014: "Didn't see Pastor Kurt, who always gives me a Lutheran Hug, which is to say the tips of your pinky fingers touching for half a second, that being the maximum amount of emotion and physical contact with which the culture is comfortable." http://tiny.cc/lilekshug

[66] At our neighborhood Catholic church, it was widely rumored that at the annual bazaar, teenagers were allowed to partake of wine. This was in the 1970s, before keeping minors away from alcohol became a federal issue, so it's possible the rumor was true. It may also have been a mischaracterization of the communion rite.

a Protestant thing, but a Prude one, and the Victorians were influential in the English and Northern European cultures that tend also to be Protestant.

In my estimation, the Mediterranean culture has an inside line on Orthosexuality because it doesn't reflexively tag sexual relations as icky. Or, to phrase it positively, sex and God are regarded as fully integrated and compatible. "That's actually Biblical: nothing in the creation story indicates God's displeasure with the fact of sexuality."[67] This doesn't mean anything goes; chastity is respected and dialogue encouraged through church teachings—in contrast to the denial, censorship, and legal restrictions that Prudes tend to reach for at the first sign of moral conflict. In fact, the Manual for Self-Examination (which some Christians use to prepare for confession) lists "Prudery" itself as a sin, defined as, "Fear of sex or condemnation of it as evil in itself. Refusal to seek adequate sexual instruction or the attempt to prevent others from obtaining it. Stimulation of excessive and harmful curiosity by undue secrecy. Repression of sex."

Dry counties, smoke-free zones, horror over public breast-feeding—these reactions go against basic human desires, criminalizing innocent acts, and setting the stage for hypocritical behavior. Where I grew up, we had a joke about a particular teetotaling denomination, "Wherever there's four of them, there's a fifth." It's a winking acknowledgment that rules are for appearances only. Rules frame a world we all say we want to live in, but we play by the rules only when others are watching.

In sexuality, the contradiction looks like this: We tell high-schoolers to resist their sex drive, then we adjourn to the pep rally where the hottest 17-year-old girls line up to flash

---

[67] Lowen, p. 61

thigh at all the boys. Hypocrisy makes abstinence education appear unserious.

As noted in the previous chapter, Prudes make the same mistake as the Liberators: They try to separate God from sex. In childrearing, this artificial disconnection can force a young person to "split off"[68] the sexual drive, expelling it as an "other" that returns, eventually, in an even less manageable form. We may recall the good girl who went wild in her first semester at college, or the nice guy who morphs into a sexual predator after a few drinks. As young people, they weren't allowed to acknowledge their developing sexual nature and to integrate it into their being. It remains a scary, external element, repressed but never reckoned with, and a likely cause of deep-seated depression or emotional instability.

We're organic beings no matter how much the Prudes try to deny us our nature.

Humans are ready to reproduce by their late teens. That biological fact nags not only at the Prudes, but at the entire Euro-American axis, because we've allowed our educational establishment to dumb down and drag out the schooling process at every level, convincing parents their children will fail at life unless institutionalized for 12-16 years[69]. And

---

[68] Alice Miller's book *Prisoners of Childhood* details the depression and emotional insecurity resulting when parents project emotional sterility and separateness onto their children.
[69] Today we may express astonishment that accomplished men like Louis Brandeis graduated from high school at age 14, but this was not unusual in his time. Public (and private) schools have every incentive to make this impossible, because once a student graduates, he no longer counts in obtaining annual funding. Graduate a year early, that's one year less of

universities already think of themselves as day-care centers, so they're not inclined to add real ones for students who have the audacity to marry and reproduce during their peak fertility.

Our commercial culture also works to keep individuals in an irresponsible, childlike state. While parents rightly encourage their kids to learn how to earn, budget, and save money, the fashion and entertainment industries work hardest on them to encourage frivolous spending. These same commercial interests sponsor all the mainstream TV and music, completing the image of a life worth living through conspicuous consumption. And the human mind has no defense against images.

In our economy, young people spend (and borrow) the most money ... right up until they have their first child. The message couldn't be clearer: Kids cramp your style. Put them off and live it up as long as you can.

The upshot of this is, advanced societies make it difficult for people to breed just as nature says they're supposed to.

The default solution is condoms, condoms, condoms, a.k.a. second-rate sex, where the intimate exchange of emotion-altering chemicals is blocked. That's immaterial because one thing Liberators and Prudes agree on is, a pop-up pregnancy is the worst possible outcome. That lesson seems to leave an impression, with pregnancy and childbirth widely regarded as a hindrance, burden, impediment to the consumer lifestyle, etc.[70], rather than a life-affirming investment. Men

---

"tuition." No wonder the once-common practice of letting advanced children skip a grade or two is forbidden.

[70] Pregnancy and childbirth are, of course, strenuous and change the course of one's life. So is a college degree, but we don't treat that as something to be put off or avoided.

put off marriage and women delay their first pregnancy so long that therapeutic intervention becomes their only hope.

But it's not just a personal matter. For men especially, delay and avoidance of fatherhood weakens and endangers the community. It's a demographic fact that unmarried young men are much more likely to commit violent crimes than married men. Early fatherhood also tends to draw men out of themselves, prodding them to adopt the masculine quality of sacrificing selfish interests for the greater good. When presented with their first child, they (should) get the message that it's time to sell the pimped-out showmobile and to grasp, possibly for the first time, that their very life is worth insuring. Young fathers—as opposed to bachelors or, in the vernacular, players—are more willing to volunteer for a community in which they have an interest in peace, order, and prosperity. Call it the epiphany of "Get off my lawn."

Younger parents also have more energy for child-rearing. (As an older parent, I know they'll need it.) Furthermore, every day that childbearing is delayed means one day less to spend on Earth loving one's children—and grandchildren. No one on his deathbed wishes for that.

Looking beyond one's own interests, late-starting families rarely exceed two children, which is below replacement rate. "Aging population" is a sanitary term for the unpleasant reality of too few young people to care for their elders—and not even enough tax revenue to pay someone else to do it. Small families hurt everyone, eventually. Recognizing this, childbearing begins to look like a duty, lest we burden complete strangers with caring for our helpless, aging selves. As we end up rationing the scant harvest of our own voluntary sterility, the 1976 movie *Logan's Run* seems less like science fiction and more like a prophecy.

In sum, delay and denial of our reproductive nature spawns a multiplicity of personal and social difficulties. Policy remedies for this have fallen short, mainly because it's the result of a complex of millions of individual decisions.

The answer may be for those of us who desire a sexuality more in tune with our nature to simply disengage from the mainstream culture and ignore its message of individualism, consumerism, and commercialized (read: costly) leisure. As importantly, we should help our own children recognize when they are being manipulated.

Close family relationships help protect adolescents from the lure of redemption-by-sex, while standoffishness at home seems to invite it. This is well-dramatized in a scene from *Rebel Without a Cause*, wherein the teenage Judy confronts her father over the way his physical affection has lagged just as she develops into a young woman. He rejects the accusation, and she promptly goes in search of the "bad boy" who, at least, can fulfill the role of a masculine figure who accepts her as she is. Close, healthy parental relationships produce successful, well-adjusted offspring. (This shouldn't surprise anyone; what often surprises us is how distant and/or unhealthy our present relationships can be.)

I first encountered the term "family intimacy" while reading of a journalist's clandestine visit to the totalitarian state of Cuba.[71] The government had managed to destroy family intimacy by getting family members to spy on each other. There would be no "safe zone" for honest communication, even within the home.

---

[71] Michael Totten, "Welcome to Cuba," World Affairs Journal http://tiny.cc/totten

In our own culture, the Prudes and Liberators unwittingly ally to disrupt family intimacy from different directions. The Prudes, by artificially separating sexuality from the rest of life so as to make intolerable (or at least uncomfortable) any sight, word, or touch that hints even slightly at sexuality. Mothers can't breast-feed in public; a father mustn't kiss his son; and once puberty hits, a teenage girl can no longer sit on Daddy's lap.

The Liberators, as Woodrow Wilson's comment succinctly illustrates (p. 25), work at driving wedges between parents and children, always in the guise of helping those deemed "at risk." It's become cliché to point out that in schools, it's easier for a 14-year-old to get contraceptives than an aspirin, but it's based on cases in fact. Liberators think nothing of tempting children to mistrust and disobey their parents. It's a responsibility no one has given them; they simply assume more and more of it unless they're met with active protest.

But responsibility begins at home, with individuals building bridges of communication, trust, and touch so that these needs are met early and often. Eventually, when nature dictates, these same desires necessarily point young people away from family. It should not surprise anyone that isolation, mistrust, and divorce run strongest in offspring whose family intimacy was weakest.

If the Liberators and the Prudes are both out of touch, what is to be the true grounding for all human connection? On what can we rely for our thoughts, words, and deeds?

Natural law has existed since the beginning of mankind and can continue to guide our decisions when we let it. Unlike the Prudes' code of standoffishness, and the Liberators' abandonment of wisdom, natural law has no human weaknesses. It is also one of the least-emphasized subjects in schools, and must be actively sought and taught in order to ground and strengthen each generation.

Sex: What Your Parents Didn't Tell You

7
Natural Law

Everything I like is either illegal, immoral, or fattening.

— Alexander Woollcott

For our first "date," Jennifer invited me to her townhouse for dinner. Dark-haired, fair-skinned, and athletic, Jennifer was always on the verge of laughter in our weekly staff meetings. She'd also been making eyes at me in those meetings, and again, the day we went out for lunch. Nothing felt more natural than to ask her for a date. Nothing thrilled me more than her answer: "Why not?"

After dinner, on her sofa and starting our third glass of wine, she rubbed her neck and complained of a stiffness in her shoulders that had bothered her all day.

Uh-huh. This was no mere complaint. She had just sent me an invitation to touch her.

I set my glass on the coffee table and motioned for her to turn. Kneading her trapezius muscles brought my nose close to her hair and skin. My pulse quickened. Our conversation faltered. Who were we kidding?

In a few minutes, I replaced my fingers with my lips. She tasted salty and sweet. Then she leaned into me.

Within a few more minutes, we were sideways on the couch, groping, tongue-kissing, and Jennifer's blouse was on the floor. We would test the limit right here, on our first date.

For reasons unknown to me at that moment, I paused. She teased my hair slowly; then she paused, too.

She lifted my chin.

Natural Law

"I'm not sure."

"Neither am I."

What Jennifer and I had started on the couch felt as natural as breathing and eating: A young man and woman drawn to each other, acting as nature led them.

It felt good to us; it felt right. Living on our own, with no parental or societal constraints, we felt free to pursue this encounter as far as we wanted. Two consenting adults. A bottle of wine. That's how it starts, or so the Liberators had coached us.

And yet, we stopped almost as suddenly as teenagers in a backseat lit up by the cops.

What neither of us could articulate was that we'd felt a different kind of "hand of the law" on us: the invisible hand of natural law.

When I first heard that phrase in a college philosophy class, I imagined something like "law of the jungle," or "gratification of whatever feels like a natural impulse to me."

Like maybe it's natural law that if I'm really hungry, I can eat a whole pizza by myself. Or if the girl I'm dancing with makes enough eye contact, I should take her home. As long as I'm not hurting anyone, I'm just following natural law. Seemed legit.

But I was not even close. Natural law takes a much higher role in the metaphysics of life, strong enough to intervene physically between me and Jennifer.

In his "Letter from a Birmingham Jail," Martin Luther King, Jr., appealed to natural law, calling it just, moral, and eternal regardless of man's preferences:

> A just law is a man-made code that squares with the moral law or the law of God. An unjust law is a code that is out of harmony with the moral law. To put it in the terms of St. Thomas Aquinas: An unjust law is a human law that is not rooted in eternal law and natural law.

In Rev. King's case, he found segregation to be in conflict with the laws of God, nature, and morality. Years earlier, the Allied powers who tried German war criminals at Nuremberg made the same case. Despite the defendants' pleas that they were "only following orders," and that no law books contained any "crimes against humanity," they were convicted. The upshot—RELATIVISM STOPS HERE—made the Nuremberg trials a touchstone for any future discussion of natural law. Nuremberg exposed the ends of relativism for the world to see. Natural law would continue to serve as the ultimate measure of man's laws and actions.

Since Aristotle, a number of thinkers and writers have offered definitions for natural law. I like this one: "a common[72], transcendent body of fundamental human

---

[72] I was surprised to learn that even explicitly atheistic governments (e.g., Soviet Union, China, North Korea) have defined obscenity about the same way as Christian-inspired states, and prohibit its distribution or public display. I had assumed that because such governments denied the existence of God and the afterlife, they didn't much care how their people reckoned with their sexual appetites. But possession of pornography has long been a punishable offense under regimes that also

principles that could be known through the right use of human reason."[73] In the Judeo-Christian tradition, this takes shape right up front as the Ten Commandments. But no one needs a philosopher or even God Almighty to comprehend natural law. We just know it. Christians like to say it's "written on the heart." We know it so intuitively that it's hard to articulate, like writing step-by-step instructions for how to walk on two legs. And there's little I can add to the body of writings on natural law that hasn't been covered by dozens of authors already[74].

But since I don't expect you to pause right now and crack open *Summa Theologica*[75], here's another definition, from a student of St. Thomas Aquinas:

> The natural law is a set of manufacturer's directions written into our nature so that we can discover through reason how we ought to act. [76]

Humans intuit natural law because it's built into the nature of us, and into everything around us as well. For example, trees always grow upward toward the sun, their roots branching outward to plunder the soil for nutrients and water. Their buds release a million seeds each spring because that's how the species continues. All this happens in obedience to natural law.

---

prohibit religious practice. So even where natural law's origin is denied, natural law remains.
[73] *St. Paul, the Natural Law, and Contemporary Legal Theory*, Michael Vacca, editor.
[74] For a fuller understanding of natural law, see sources listed in the Epilogue.
[75] Charles Rice's *50 Questions on the Natural Law* provides an excellent introduction.
[76] Ibid.

But the moral difference between humans and trees is, the tree can't choose any different. As self-directed beings with free will, we can go against our nature. We could even force the tree to break natural law by, say, re-engineering its DNA so it grows upside-down. In that case, the tree would die.

Humans who break natural law usually die, too, although we can often buy our way out of it. By the time we're adults, we've already learned how. So we tend to think of natural law as optional, especially when we want something as attractive as sex.

To put this into practice, we must identify the building blocks of natural law: means and ends.

Any thing or action is a means or an end. An end can also be called a good, or a product or goal. It's what the means leads to.

When a child asks the simple question, "Why?" that shows he's starting to think in terms of natural law. He's identified the means; now he's asking what end is served by it.[77]

---

[77] Parents help children grow in their native understanding of natural law partly with the help of legend and mythology. "The Boy Who Cried Wolf" isn't a factual story—we can't look up the livestock records or the coroner's report for the shepherd boy (in the original, he's killed by the wolf), but the legend tells of a natural law: Don't abuse the trust of others. In other words, don't bear false witness. In this and in most natural-law legends, the consequence of violating the law is death, or at least a close brush with it. We call these "morality tales." Adults like them, too. TV shows like *Fantasy Island* told stories of what happens when we actually get our way in everything. It doesn't end well, except you get to leave when it's over ... because you're rich.

It may be needless to say, but a person must never be a means to someone's end. Yet, as complex, selfish, and sometimes warped beings, our most frequent violation of natural law is to use another person as a means. They will know it's wrong, and they'll resent it. They call it "feeling used." This is exactly how one feels after serving as someone else's sexual scratching post. But it's not just a feeling; it's a fact. The feeling simply points to where it hurts.

In Liberator thinking, natural law goes out the window when both parties agree, in advance, to be used as means. The phrase "two consenting adults in the privacy of their own home" captures this nicely, as well as the more modern "friends with benefits." Surely there can be no wrong if both partners consent.

But despite all the Liberators' assurances, something doesn't quite feel right about this. I sensed it on Jennifer's couch even though neither of us could articulate it. In all of our upbringing, no one had helped us make the connection between natural law and sex. According to our culture, those two had nothing to do with one another. Sex was something adults could do whenever they wanted.

So why didn't we go ahead? Which of the "Thou shalt nots"—the common, transcendent body of fundamental human principles—were we tripping over?

On reflection, I'd say it was the one about coveting your neighbor's wife. Of course, Jennifer wasn't married, and neither was I. But I also had no plans to marry her. She could very well end up as another man's wife. And I would not only have coveted her, I'd have exploited her in a way that her eventual husband would not want to think about.

Neither would I, especially if he were my boss, neighbor, or customer. In a six-billion-inhabitant world, I could probably put enough distance between us so we would never meet. But even then, we're only a page apart on Facebook. And spiritually, we would be brothers.[78]

There's a word to summarize the thorny consequences of violating natural law: shame[79]. Not an uncommon feeling on the morning after a casual encounter. Of course, if Jennifer and I had been married, we'd have nothing to be ashamed of. We would only feel embarrassed if, say, we'd forgotten to close the curtains.

At the heart of all this is a truth: There are no purely physical sex acts. Sex is loaded with meanings. Metaphysics ensures the place of meaning in human relationships.

Interestingly, I haven't met anyone who, once he understands natural law, believes himself exempt from it. However, we all think we can bend natural law—just as we can roll very, very slowly past a STOP sign—because there's no chance of arrest by "natural police" nor of getting sued for damages by "natural lawyers." And again, we can usually get away with it if we have enough wealth, which most people in modern societies do.

---

[78] This is why nobody likes the player. We may envy his ability to get the girls. But he's not liked. Your girl might be his next conquest. As a humorist once wrote of Bill Clinton, "He wants all the girls, but he also wants the guys to like him."

[79] There's a critical difference between our senses of shame and embarrassment. Shame is rooted in an unresolved conflict between thought, word, or deed that distorts your personality; it doesn't hinge on what others see or think. Embarrassment results from exposure to others; its morality is irrelevant. It wouldn't be shameful to accidentally expose your privates. It would be shameful to show them intentionally.

This wasn't always so. In hunter-gatherer times, when everyone had to beat things with rocks just to eat, a woman conceiving a child out of wedlock could wind up exiled. Of course that's a harsh sentence, but to fearful villagers living hand-to-mouth, it made sense: a fatherless child put yet another burden on everyone's limited resources, and with enough little bastards running around the place would soon turn into a ghetto, making it vulnerable to attack and pillage by better-disciplined peoples from over the next hill. A rash of unwed motherhood could get everyone killed.[80]

But today, an Octomom can choose single parenthood in the knowledge that she can rely on morally blind public assistance, or earn enough money to pay someone else to do her mothering while she goes on hunting and gathering. Since our meat now comes in cellophane packages, there's no need for an aggressive male to hunt down, kill, and skin the occasional wildebeest, either. The children will be kept indoors and fed, at minimum. No one's actual survival is in jeopardy.

---

[80] There are other laws like this. It pained me to realize (late but not too late) that choosing not to have children violates natural law, because it leaves no one to care for us when we're old. Unless we build unusually strong relationships with other family and friends, choosing against procreation is tantamount to depending on strangers for one's care. Of course, if we make enough money to salt away a small fortune, we can at least be assured of admittance to a facility where nonrelatives will show some degree of charity in feeding us and changing our diapers. This is costly, however, and if we don't save enough of our own money we will have to compel others through taxation or mercy to keep us bathed and balmed. Visit your county home for the elderly to see how this looks. Even that arrangement may grow impossible when a whole generation grows too small to pay for it.

Or think of it this way: If you choose not to have children, you will be the first in your line throughout human history to do so, as well as the last.

So there's one natural law break—the link between sex and family structure—that can be ignored, as long as we have enough money.

But just as we say it's a miscarriage of justice for a criminal's high-dollar lawyers to get him off the hook, so it is when we buy our way out of natural law. If I sire a child out of wedlock, I can afford an abortion. Or I could ditch my aging wife for a nubile twentysomething, if I pay the old lady off and send the kids along with her. This is why so many "victimless" crimes like adultery aren't prosecuted, or even prosecutable: they run square up against what wealthy and powerful people want for themselves. Their demand—"I want it this way"—cannot be reasoned with. Natural law is pure reason.

At heart, humans don't like rules. To have more options than we'd ever need, even if we don't use them, helps us to feel free. We seek the feeling of freedom. But that feeling can be deceptive. In reality, natural law is freedom.

The law about coveting your neighbor's goods, for example—think about how it feels to see your neighbor drive up in his brand-new Infiniti. The one with the heated seats that memorize individual settings and positions. That can be an awful feeling, to realize you may never, ever make enough money to buy one of those for yourself, even on credit. And if you can't let go of that, you'll go to your grave with it, maybe decades later, at the end of a life spent gnashing teeth over your misfortune.

Even though you're free to feel this way, it's not freedom; it's the opposite, slavery. Your envy owns you, and it can

Natural Law

take you out back and beat you bloody every day for no reason other than your own unwillingness to let it go.

But if you can let it go, then you no longer care what your neighbor rides around in, and neither do you care what anyone else thinks of your own driveasaur. Then you're free to appreciate your friend's good fortune, confident in the knowledge that you're no better and no worse for it. No longer a slave to envy. I've known people like that, and they're the happiest humans I've ever met. Mainly because they're rational about themselves and others.

Natural law is rational. In fact, that's the Cliff's Notes version: Be rational. It's our human weakness, our desire to have our own way in everything, that's irrational. Judeo-Christians call this original sin. And because it's a weakness, it's what the enemies of rational thinking always go to work on when they want to persuade us to put their interests above ours. Marketing people, I'm looking at you. And at me, too, because I've worked in marketing. I've made a living convincing others they should give my client their disposable income. Or, if ready cash isn't available, to run up debt so they can buy whatever we're selling. This isn't rational behavior.

Obedience to natural law frees us from slavery to corrupting forces. In the end, we're going to obey something. It might as well be something right.

So, how do you know what's right? One pretty good indicator is whether the anticipation is better than the outcome.

Porn's a good example. No man continues to browse porn sites after ejaculating. In fact, he usually wants nothing to do with porn for a while.

Gluttony of any sort fits this bill. A third helping of lasagna is rarely a good idea, but anticipation can block the memory of that last bellyache.

Natural law endures. We can dismiss it, or call it outdated, or pretend it doesn't apply to us, but we can't rewrite or wish it away. We can choose to live within it, though, and find life's highway more enjoyable when we stay off the guardrails.

And perhaps the best aspect of natural law is that no one can take it from us. Liberators can deceive, Prudes can deny, but ultimately, their fantasies of controlling us break up against the reality that we can govern ourselves. To do so competently and without despising ourselves for our inevitable errors, we need to understand that even wrong choices don't make us bad people—just confused as to the difference between higher goods and lower goods.

8
Higher Goods, Lower Goods

The most painful moral struggles are not those between good and evil, but between good and a lesser good.

—Barbara Grizzuti Harrison

I stepped into Office Depot for some paper but before I could pass the checkout counter I nearly hurt myself.

A splendid young thing, a trainee, smiled at me as I passed. Maybe 20, max. Caramel skin and light brown hair. I walked past her in a flash, but her image went right through me.

The "nearly hurt" was from fighting my head to keep it on straight. I have no business gawking at a girl like that.

I kept walking. Straight to the paper. Trying to find 28-lb. white, which is a rare stock. Finally got it; a reasonable price? Not really, but I needed it.

And what about ... that? Did I need that?

I knew I'd have to pass her again, at close range. How would I handle it?

Then I saw myself in a mirror.

My black, wool topcoat enhanced my height and shoulders. It also brought out the gray in my temples. And that's what I saw foremost in the mirror.

So, instead of approaching the counter as a slave to my eyes, I would demonstrate how a 40-something father conducts himself in the presence of a beautiful young woman.

I have two daughters. This is what I want them to see from men, too.

Every man, married, engaged, or otherwise spoken for, runs into similar situations from time to time. They can eat at him more or less, depending on his state of emotion, spirit, and/or intoxication. (Perhaps, even, location. At a national convention, I heard a female attendee say, "Some men come to these things and act like they're not married.")

A man feels this pull not because he wants to leave his wife for an attractive stranger, friend, or co-worker, but perhaps because it simply feels good to flirt. It's like a trip to the gym after you've missed a couple of appointments. Muscles you hadn't worked in a while get infused with fresh blood. It's a good burn.

To the Liberators, it's an invitation. Maybe the wife would be up for an open relationship. Since natural law is only a construct (like marriage itself), all we need is a waiver. Might as well ask her. It's biology, you know: Like the other primates, human males are hard-wired to spread their genes.

To the Prudes—whom we're more likely to hear in our heads—it's an abomination. Isn't there some kind of switch a man can throw when he says "I do"? Why can't a married man be repelled by other women the way we're all put off by others' flatulence?

In confronting a situation like this, we may commit yet another error: to be so concerned with our upstanding self-image that we simply cannot abide both the temptation and the self-condemnation. Pride being central to all the sins, we simply split this emotion off from our personality. That's unhealthy, and it will return, and we won't be any more prepared to manage it later.[81]

---

[81] A friend calls this "Mr. North Dallas Syndrome" for the idea that both

To deal with irrationality in a more rational way, we must realize that we need not be monsters to take the wrong path from time to time. We know the obvious evils: serial murder, shoplifting, truancy. It's in the less stark and certain areas that we wrestle with ourselves because we're hazy on the difference between higher goods and lower goods.

Returning to the example above, flirting isn't inherently evil. It's how I met my wife, so it can be a good of some sort. What makes it a lower good in this situation is the circumstances: I am a married man who loves and wants a close relationship with my wife. I can't have that at the same time I'm entertaining other women.

Let's look at another example of lower goods and higher goods, from a legend we all used to know.

In the Garden of Eden, the devil tempts Eve with godlike knowledge. In and of itself, that knowledge is a good. But in Eve's case, she would have to trade a higher good for it. That higher good was obedience to God, who had instructed her to leave that knowledge alone. But Eve took the lower good, sacrificing the higher one. She couldn't obey God and still acquire the forbidden knowledge.

Most every wrongful act fits this formula. We get gratification from lower goods, but only until we realize we've lost something higher. Of course, we can simply deny the tradeoff through the power of human rationalization. But deep down, we know we've made a bad bargain. That

---

he and his respectable circles view him as "better" than his deep-seated desires.

works on our conscience and it will eventually show in our countenance, too.[82]

To return to my encounter with the sales clerk: Flirting isn't wrong in itself until it costs me a higher good, which in this case is an honest and open relationship with my wife. Imagine me coming home that afternoon to her smile and the question, "How was your day?"

I would not be able to tell her the truth: That the high point was chatting up a hot young woman. So I would have to say something else, and there goes the honest, open relationship I actually value more than the attention of a pretty girl. To cover my sin, I would have to lead a double life, a stressful deception where I would lock away parts of myself and take care never to divulge them, even by accident.

We distinguish between higher goods and lower goods for our sanity, and not—as the Liberators do—to blur the lines between good and evil. The distinction helps us work more realistically with the choices we make every minute. Choosing a lower good over a higher one doesn't make us into evil beings; it makes us human, capable of both reason and of disregarding it in moments of temptation. As Charles Darwin phrased it, "The highest possible stage in moral culture is when we recognize that we ought to control our thoughts."

This kind of clarity makes the concepts of good and evil less daunting, especially in matters of the heart such as sexuality. Once we understand that our sexual nature is integrated

---

[82] The classic movie *The Picture of Dorian Gray* makes excellent use of imagery for this.

with our spiritual, we can more reliably deal with its day-to-day resurfacing. In the case of my encounter with the sales clerk, her good looks still captured my attention; I simply chose a purposeful rather than an instinctive response in the end. There was no cause for condemnation of myself as inherently evil simply because I had to make that choice.

Decisions like that may come before us almost daily. Our sexual nature affects every relationship, whether professional or personal, lifelong or fleeting. It even affects our relationship with images, setting up conflicts unavoidable in the age of touch-screen technology and worldwide access.

9
Masturbation & Porn

I count him braver who overcomes his desires than him who conquers his enemies, for the hardest victory is over self.

—Aristotle

My 11th-grade best friend Eddie and I lacked the social skills we needed to learn about life except through trial-and-error. We channeled our teenage recklessness into trying out all the wrong answers, with little to lose socially because nobody paid attention to us.

We didn't actually set out to do stupid things; but with driver's licenses and permission to be out in the city at night, our potential for mischief occasionally hit teen-comedy levels.

One night, our curiosity about all things sexual drove us to see for ourselves what lay between the windowless walls of an "adult arcade." We had a pretty good idea what the three Xs on the sign meant, but we wanted confirmation. One Saturday night, we parked out back of the cinder-block building and entered through a metal door.

A wall of pornographic magazines greeted us, sealed with shrink wrap and Day-Glo price tags. A display case off to one side held a collection of what we guessed, by their fleshy-looking parts, to be sex toys. Atop the counter stood neat boxes of little amyl nitrate and nitrous-oxide capsules. No clue what those were for, but we'd seen lots of empties rolling around in the parking lot.

On the opposite wall, two separate doors appeared to serve as entry and exit to some netherworld, one door with a knob and the other without. Naturally, we went for the doorknob, only to be interrupted by the clerk behind the display case.

"You're gonna need quarters to go in there," he droned, looking us over before reaching for the cash register. We dutifully handed over dollar bills and took our change.

The clerk pressed a button and the door buzzed. The solenoid lock gave me pause—I'd only heard those in secure areas, and the sound made me think our escape options might be limited—but Eddie had already opened the door. I followed, determined not to be left alone in this place no matter what.

We entered a dim corridor with black floors, black ceilings, and black plywood walls. The smell made a bigger impression than the décor, though: an admixture of locker-room and Pine-Sol.

Along one side of the corridor we gawked at tacked-up mini-posters of stills from porn flicks, each with a large numeral artlessly stapled to it. Peering farther down the hall, we could make out a labyrinth of numbered doors.

And for the first time in my young life I grasped the feeling of "eyes upon me." In the shadowy corners of the labyrinth, older men stood hands-in-pockets, faces hidden in the dark but unmistakably watching me and Eddie. At the right time of year, this would have made a great haunted house, except for the smell.

Without a word, Eddie and I chose our respective pornos and set off separately. I ducked through a numbered door and locked it behind me.

Once my eyes adjusted, I spotted a glowing coin slot and dropped a quarter into it. A small screen lit up before me, and there I stood watching my first actual porn movie, a faded, 16mm silent production with subtitles. In a short time, my close-up view of sexual congress triggered a familiar response in my groin, and, unable to think about dealing with that in these weird surrounds, I let my mind and eyes wander.

The eight-foot walls around me spired into dark, open space. As I looked around the booth, my eyes adjusted enough to make out that the plywood right next to me had been altered. There was a hole in it, several inches in diameter, just below waist level.

I noticed light flickering through the hole, suggesting that the guy next door was having his own cinematic experience. Then I saw fingers through the hole. Just below waist level. Then the fingers beckoned.

Back in the labyrinth, Eddie and I nearly ran over each other, having gotten the same sight about the same time. We fast-walked out, squinting in the fully lit lobby, past the wall o' porn and the clerk and his display case, and out the main door into the parking lot. We scrambled into the car and roared off, laughing with a mix of discomfort and disappointment, out of breath from our mad rush to escape and still grasping at what kind of bizarre side of adult life we'd just gotten a glimpse of.

Eddie and I didn't talk much about that experience with each other, and certainly not with anyone else. One realization, however, which we shared in the form of a one-sentence exchange, would add to our nascent understanding of real-life sexuality. It was the epiphany that no female outside of a mental institution would begin to consider taking part in what was routine in that place.

Not many men would, either, but the whole back-alley scene certainly caught the public's attention as AIDS became a household word, and again when a local, prominent newspaper columnist got arrested in another arcade for propositioning an undercover cop. What would drive any man to such depths?

It's for the same reason, different only in degree, that men shell out billions of dollars for pornography, lap dances, and bar bills for females they do not know: Men just aren't as sexually sophisticated as women. [83]

As noted earlier, Dustin Hoffman once aptly compared being a young man to "waking up every day chained to a maniac."

Even as a five-year-old, I remember sneaking off with my sister's copy of *Seventeen* so I could stare, in private, at the full-cover close-up of Susan Dey.[84] Nothing sexual, of course. I was just smitten.[85]

---

[83] "[W]omen don't tend to stare at men's bodies. We tend to stare at the same stuff men stare at: women's bodies. It's not because most women have latent lesbian fantasies; it's because women are attracted to the idea of being wanted far more than we are by simply watching naked men. Women don't ogle. They dream." Sheila Wray Gregoire, *The Good Girl's Guide to Great Sex*.
[84] *The Partridge Family* Susan Dey, not *L.A. Law* Susan Dey.
[85] I've noticed this happen even to married men my age. A guy next to me will be staring at a woman he thinks I might know, and whisper, "What's her name?" The tone is unmistakable. He won't do anything with her name, of course. He just wants to talk about a woman who has,

But in my middle teens, stronger forces came to bear on my body and brain, and I started paying much closer attention to the way my female classmates looked, moved, and smelled. Then I experienced the captivating kiss and feel of a real, young woman. Every man remembers how that first slow dance changed everything.

In young adulthood, having never been instructed on how to master this powerful new impulse, I felt out of control. My decisionmaking suffered from a focus on attracting, and attractive, girls. I wasn't alone in this; some guys seemed better able to conceal their hunger. But we all felt it and did all we could think of, and could afford, to accommodate our primal urge to ejaculate inside an attractive female.

George Gilder described the core difference between men and women as one of "sexual sophistication," in which women have the advantage. (This does not mean every man is less sexually sophisticated than every woman. Rather, it's a generalization that holds true in most cases, making it a truth.) Gilder cites the observations of Kinsey colleague Mary Jane Sherfey that "women can both enjoy sexual relations more profoundly and durably *and forgo them more easily* than can men"[86] (emphasis added). For a woman, "intercourse is only one of many sex acts or experiences. Her breasts and her womb symbolize a sex role that extends, at least as a potentiality, through pregnancy, childbirth, lactation, suckling, and long-term nurture. Rather than a brief performance, female sexuality is a long, unfolding process...."[87] Again, from Gilder:

> The man, on the other hand, has just one sex act and he is exposed to conspicuous failure in it.

---

for the moment, captivated him.
[86] Gilder, p. 9
[87] Ibid.

> His erection is a mysterious endowment that he can never fully understand or control.[88]

Men's relative lack of sexual sophistication is the main reason that in most places, females can't legally go bare-breasted in public. Only one of the sexes is wired so hot as to react physically to the mere sight of the other shirtless.[89]

Today, such images—and much, much more—come at us through an invisible pipeline called the Internet, which follows us around every waking hour, ready to prime our hunger. It also leaves women wondering what the hell has happened to men over the past 20 years.[90]

In 1970, a presidential commission concluded the public was making too much fuss over porn, finding no "evidence that exposure to explicit sexual materials adversely affects character or moral attitudes regarding sex and sexual conduct."[91] The report was DOA in Congress, which took the more realistic view that the entire purpose of pornography is to accelerate orgasm in masturbating males, and that not much redeeming value could come of that.

---

[88] Gilder, pp. 10-11

[89] Most Liberators bristle over the fact that male and female have profoundly different perspectives on sex. This doesn't mesh well with crude equality theories. I'd expect them to get it when confronted with another of these routine cases of a teenage boy caught "sexting" a picture of his penis to a girl. Propriety is an issue, of course, but the salient point is, only a fool of a male would expect a female to get hot-n-bothered over a penis shot. That they don't must keep the Liberators perpetually puzzled.

[90] See "Why Does He Prefer Porn over Me?" *Psychology Today* blog: http://tiny.cc/vqckhx

[91] *Report of the Commission on Obscenity and Pornography*, 1970.

Simply put, most people saw porn for what it is: junk food for the male sexual appetite.

In our present age, it may seem quaint that the government ever bothered to take up the matter of pornography, which currently whizzes around our heads wirelessly in volumes hard to imagine. But at that time, filming people having sex and showing that to other people was a phenomenon. Regular folks were deeply concerned over the commercial exploitation of a private, sublime act. They urged law enforcement to prosecute distributors of porn on charges of obscenity, which courts struggled to define[92], and which automatically became a federal matter if the U.S. Postal Service was involved in shipping the finished product. Pornographers claimed First Amendment protection, prefacing every release with a (literal) flag-waving appeal to their audience's patriotism, in the event they ever be called to serve as a juror in an obscenity case.

Eventually, district attorneys would tire of pressing charges against the flood of porn, and turned their limited attention toward the growing, violent-crime problem. The Internet would replace the mail, and prosecutions became pointless, like trying to exterminate a forest for termites.

And in the '70s, the Liberators declared the only possible downside of masturbation—porn-fueled or otherwise—was guilt. In unchaining our hands, they mocked even the etymology of masturbation, which is, "self pollution." What could possibly be harmful about touching your own body?

---

[92] The need to spell out legal definitions of obscenity gave the Liberators an ideal opportunity to inject relativist thinking. Supreme Court Justice Potter Stewart stepped on the mine with his memorable phrase, "I know it when I see it," which opened the door for the "contemporary community standards" analysis, which led to the notion that what was obscene in one city or state might not be in another.

They said we were just practicing for real sex, harmlessly bleeding off tension that could otherwise make us unhappy, or even drive us to rape. President Clinton's Surgeon General famously advocated masturbation as an alternative to the temptations of unsafe sex. The Liberators pointed to her dismissal as proof that our uptight society still wasn't ready to deal with reality.

About that time, the World Wide Web made its way into homes, with the power to deliver in seconds more hardcore porn than any human had seen in a lifetime. Virtually all of it was aimed at males, the only audience willing to pay for it. With a firehose of hardcore filling so many hard drives, the Surgeon General's dream could at last be realized, a nation of porn-abetted wankers, shades drawn and pants around their ankles, happily spilling their sexual frustrations into the laundry.

But in time, real women in the real world started to get strange feedback from males gorging on the stuff. "Facial" became a gift no longer suitable for Mother's Day. Pubic hair, a sign of sexual maturity since the dawn of man, started getting bad reviews. The new normal would include liberated, college-age males publicly chanting, "No means yes/Yes means anal."[93]

If porn-fueled masturbation is supposed to make young men less of a threat to females, there's no evidence of it. More importantly, porn appears to make men less adaptable as boyfriends or husbands. In Utah, men buy more online

---

[93] From "Yale fraternity pledges chant about rape," Salon, Oct. 15, 2010 http://tiny.cc/yalepledges Of course, frat boys have a reputation for outrageous acts done solely to out-do each other, or as rites of passage. This chant, however, betrays not only a lack of imagination, but familiarity with an act that degrades all participants—including the voyeur.

pornography per capita than in any other state. Salt Lake City also employs more cosmetic surgeons per capita than any of the 50 largest U.S. cities.[94] Porn appears to be doing for silicone what Marilyn Monroe did for peroxide.

The reason? The human mind has no defense against images. When young men's daily exposure to sexuality consists of hairless young women shaped like pool toys and obsessed with semen collection, what can we expect men's real-life desires to start looking like?

Ironically, the same technology that has put porn into mass distribution now facilitates a rebellion against it. A subculture of young men is calling itself to order online. They aren't interested in the porn industry's latest exploitation of yet another 18-year-old victim of paternal neglect.[95] Rather, they want to get away from her, and from the whole world of masturbatory voyeurism.

They've discovered that after years of holding their own, so to speak, they can't function in the presence of a live female,[96]

---

[94] From "America's Vainest Cities," Forbes, Nov. 29, 2007 http://tiny.cc/plasticsurgerySLC. I'm not singling out Utah for any particular reason, other than it seems no coincidence that these two statistics would point to the same population.

[95] In researching this, I learned it's not unheard-of for the start of a porn shoot to be delayed when the female "star" is discovered crying. Also, the average career for a porn star lasts two years.

[96] Erectile dysfunction aside, the practice of a young man's hurrying his own climax along—crucial to minimize the chance of getting caught masturbating—remains in the sexual reflexes, fouling up the timeless interactions and waypoints that lead to true orgastic release. Climaxing quickly in this fire-drill mode, or failing to ejaculate at all in the presence of his girl, he aborts their natural synergy. She's left to wonder if she somehow contributed to his dysfunction.

a stunning example of the metaphysical foretelling the physical. Accidentally, they came across one of Islam's lesser-known "uncleans": the "sweat of an unlawful ejaculation."[97] They've learned that what they'd been told was harmless actually makes them smell bad, feel bad, and act bad. They've tasted death, and they're repelled by it. It turns out that adultery—another word for contamination, or the self-pollution we were warned about—can happen to an individual, as well as to a couple.

These young men seek support from one another in forums promoted not by religious bodies, but by themselves, based on a growing body of research on the self-destructive brain chemistry activated by pornography. They see "The Demise of Guys"[98] and start to grasp what the hell is happening to them.

Once they zero in on masturbation (a.k.a. "fapping") as the source of their problems, their testimonials run nothing short of plaintive:[99]

- It seemed obvious that if I stopped objectifying women I would think clearer around them, be more focused and be able to form a healthy relationship, instead of many loose ones.
- To prove that I own my urges not the other way around.
- Because women are so much more interesting—and somehow so much sexier—when I'm not fapping.
- Because I'm tired of walking hand-in-hand with my girlfriend thinking that I'm slowly cutting at the veins of our relationship when she's not around.

---

[97] *Little Green Book: Sayings of the Ayatollah Khomeini*, cited in Mark Steyn's column, "The Shagged Sheep" http://tiny.cc/shaggedsheep
[98] Available on YouTube.
[99] Comments copied from online discussion forums.

- So that I can feel closer to my wife, have integrity, and enjoy the small things in life more. So tired of walking around dazed and bored and blah all the time.
- I am actually fapping to a dream, to a fantasy. Something that isn't there, something that sometimes is really degrading to women. This action felt degrading for me.[100]
- I felt pathetic for being controlled by my desires, instead of being the one in control.

Apparently, the Surgeon General never bothered to validate her prescription.

Note one commenter's wording: "own my urges." This is neither the Prudes' "Don't touch that!" nor the Liberators' "Go for it!" but the more Judeo-Christian "Acknowledge that something you're attracted to isn't good for you, and take responsibility for your actions."[101] Here, in the safe anonymity of online exchanges, they've rediscovered the confessional.

Once they recognize their state, these men find they can turn away from what they'd been told was freedom but was slavery in disguise. They terminate their double life,[102] free from the stress of keeping an online fantasy world separate from the real one.

---

[100] As other testimonials bear out, nobody really likes masturbating with porn. Every male does the same thing just after he's done: "Alt-F4," completing a kind of mental bulimia.

[101] Not as explicit a commandment as the Ten, this teaching can be gleaned from comprehensive study of the Bible.

[102] Anecdotes suggest it's common practice in today's military for a fallen soldier's buddies to scrub the porn off his hard drive before his belongings are sent to next of kin.

Most commonly, they escape temptation through the pursuit of fitness, sports training, and the camaraderie of their fellows. In other words, the same world that able-bodied boys and young men inhabited before the television set—and later, the game console and Web-enabled computer—lured them indoors and changed them from builders of civilization into spectators.[103] From Gilder:

> Particularly in a society where clear and affirmative masculine activities are scarce, men may feel a compulsive desire to perform their one unquestionable male role. It is only when men are engaged in a relentless round of masculine activities in the company of males—Marine Corps training is one example—that their sense of manhood allows them to avoid sex without great strain.[104]

And, per Prof. Budziszewski, "A man, like a woman, is correctly defined only when he is positively defined" or:[105]

> the best instance of a human male is not a glorified, walking packet of urges, but a man who, for the sake of the highest and greatest goods, commands himself, strengthens his brothers, and defends his sisters, regarding even the meanest of women as a lady.[106]

Outside of the military, Boy Scouts of America is the largest organization to positively define masculinity, ensuring it will remain a target of the Liberators through its co-opting and

---

[103] Here's a biblical example of how idleness enables delinquency: King David commits a murder-by-proxy after using his spare time to gawk at a married woman bathing outdoors. (Was this the ancients' equivalent of looking too long at the *Sports Illustrated* swimsuit issue?)
[104] Gilder, p. 11
[105] Budziszewski, p. 58
[106] Ibid., p. 64

destruction.[107] Liberators cannot tolerate the promotion of masculine values.

The Prudes treated masturbation as a mental illness with bodily consequences, going so far as to adopt forcible circumcision of boys in an effort to tamp down their sex drive.[108] The Liberators took a similarly mechanistic view, convincing young men that self-induced ejaculation is simply routine maintenance for the genitals. There's no scientific basis that either of these approaches achieves its intent, but they're neat rationalizations, and they preclude self-denial and self-improvement—key components of masculinity.

The British coined the term "wanker" to describe a male who fecklessly serves himself. One need not be a metaphysician to see that the sexual powers were meant to take us out of ourselves, not turn us inward.

So, where to from here?

At this point it's neither politically nor technologically feasible to stanch the Internet pornucopia. So the answer to temptation will have to be like the one prescribed for most other unhealthy indulgences, like cocaine, complex carbs, or console games: Get up and go outside.

Women can help this along by refusing to accept porn's corruption of the men they would like to have court and marry them. No more razor burn in the pubic area. No

---

[107] BSA is already hobbled. As of this writing, and for the first time, parents have to consider whether to allow their sons to share tents and showers with openly homosexual peers.
[108] "The operation should be performed by a surgeon without administering an anesthetic, as the brief pain attending the operation will have a salutary effect upon the mind, especially if it be connected with the idea of punishment." http://tiny.cc/harveyk

more playing along with ghastly ideas in the bedroom, or for that matter, the operating room. No more pleading e-mails to sex columnists for smarmy reassurances that their man's browser history has absolutely no impact on the relationship.

To women, I caution that refusal must be done tactfully, realizing that porn (actually any form of female nudity) short-circuits the male conscience much as that basket of warm tortilla chips undermines the Atkins plan. Speak in love: It's a deeply shameful subject for him. (That's why he runs from it when he's finished.)[109]

But as in dating, dancing, and marriage proposals, in order for this change of attitude to spread, men will have to lead, perhaps by building communities online and off to show themselves and one another who owns them.[110]

---

[109] 1 Corinthians 16:14: "Let all that you do be done in love."
[110] Example: http://tiny.cc/menfightback

10
Talking to Your Children

Listen earnestly to anything your children want to tell you, no matter what. If you don't, they won't tell you the big stuff when they are big, because to them it has always been big stuff.

— Catherine M. Wallace

> *My first year out of college I shared a house with several other recent graduates. We quickly learned that we all liked to drink and tell stories, so in getting to know each other we spent many a late night in the living room trading tales from our most recent common experience, the university life.*
>
> *I quickly discovered that my housemates' sexual histories were vastly more colorful than mine. In college, they'd participated in a kind of sexual musical chairs, where willing females presented themselves one after another to the most desirable males until the music eventually stopped and everyone graduated.*
>
> *I felt I'd missed out, having failed to attract very many girls in school, so I urged the guys on in their storytelling. As the beer flowed, they started to one-up each other. Dave took the unofficial first prize when he acknowledged bedding three girls simultaneously. Another got our admiration for his audacity to request and receive oral sex in the back seat of a car ... with his buddies up front, pretending not to notice.*

> *Fast-forward 25 years. Dave and I live far from each other, with wives and children. I caught up with him by phone one evening. He said his elder daughter was about to graduate from high school, and the two were scheduling a campus tour of the East Coast. She planned to enroll in the autumn.*
>
> *I thought about that for a minute.*
>
> *"Dave," I asked, "What happens when she meets a guy like you were?"*

Perhaps you've turned to this chapter first because it's about what keeps you up at night. As a father, that's what keeps me up, too.

Maybe you picked up this book because you got word that your teenage son sexted a girl with a picture of his genitals, and you're wondering what you're supposed to do about that. Or maybe your daughter did something just as appalling, and you have no clue what led to it.

The culture around us has become a minefield, and no one seems to have a map. At the least, I want my kids to come to me for direction. Hence, the lead-off quote.

So if you've jumped right here as your starting point, I heartfully recommend that you read the previous chapters first. Like anyone, I'm attracted to the quick-fix, shortcut, bottom line. But I was not equipped to understand, let alone write about, Orthosexuality until I shook off half a lifetime of cultural misdirection on natural law, masculinity and femininity, and the true meaning of sexual freedom. For most of my life I didn't realize my generation existed on a metaphysical battleground in the war between Prudes and Liberators, and I could not articulate how it felt to wake up every day "chained to a maniac." A better grounding in first principles would have saved me years of puzzlement and hurt.

Living away from nature as most of us do, we can grow up without an earthy foundation that helps us see sexuality as a normal part of life.

One day at a local park, I noticed a mother suddenly leap onto a swingset to distract her kids from the sight of two squirrels mating nearby.

I couldn't help but think this would have made a 19th Century farm wife laugh out loud: "Your young ones don't know that animals mate?"

The organic understanding that sexual energy is directly connected to procreation can also be blocked by the Prudes' censorship and confused by the Liberators' efforts to separate sexuality from its life-affirming and -renewing side.

Add in the exploitative sexual imagery in entertainment, advertising, and literature, and you have the potential for a generation to come of age believing sex is a mysterious source of gratification, the ultimate answer to adolescent longing, a cure-all for feelings of loneliness, a validation of who we are and want to be.

Here's how all that misdirection adds up:

- More than 40 percent of parents don't talk to their kids about sex until after they are sexually active.[111]

---

[111] *Pediatrics*, January 1, 2010 http://tiny.cc/donttalk

- As early as 2004, 57 percent of 9-19 year-olds had seen online porn.[112] (Note that this study took place before the spread of wi-fi enabled smart phones.)
- More than one-third of teenage Internet users report involuntary exposure to pornography.[113]
- A growing body of evidence shows porn viewing damages one's ability to connect physically with an actual mate.[114]
- In 10 out of 12 developed nations with available data, more than two thirds of teens have had sex.[115]
- Watching TV shows with sexual content apparently hastens the initiation of teen sexual activity. Sexual talk on TV has the same effect on teens as depictions of sex.[116]
- A poll of college students[117] shows an increasingly casual attitude about hookups, or sex with casual dates/pickups/friends. Perhaps this is a consequence of "safe sex" education's emphasis on microbes over metaphysics. (44 percent reported that one of their sexual partners during the past year was a casual date/pickup, or a friend [68.6 percent]).
- Recent studies of brain chemistry indicate that having multiple sex partners impairs one's ability to form a long-term, monogamous relationship.[118]
- Almost 41 percent of children in the U.S. are born to unmarried mothers.[119]

---

[112] London School of Economics (PDF file) http://tiny.cc/teenseen
[113] *Pediatrics*, February 1, 2007 http://tiny.cc/damagemate
[114] http://www.yourbrainonporn.com
[115] "Teenage Births in Rich Nations," UNICEF, 2001 (PDF download) http://tiny.cc/teenbirths
[116] "Does Watching Sex on Television Influence Teens' Sexual Activity?" Rand Corporation, 2004 http://tiny.cc/sexontv
[117] Monto and Carey, University of Portland, 2013 http://tiny.cc/casualpoll
[118] McIlhaney and Bush, location 482
[119] "Unmarried Childbearing," Centers for Disease Control, 2012, http://tiny.cc/cdcunmarried

Perhaps the first truth we have to acknowledge is, sex education cannot just be a talk. An awkward half-hour at the kitchen table won't substitute for parental modeling and genuine relationship-building. Nor can it counteract what the culture, peers, and marketing forces throw at young people every waking hour.

I'm hardly a well-experienced or insightful parent, but I have learned this much: Nothing is more important than the quality of the relationship. Perhaps this is especially critical in sexual relations, since they cannot be demonstrated, only implied.

There's an old saying that nobody dies regretting too much time spent with one's children. It's in relationship-building that we realize how different each child can be in learning style, temperament, and personality. With that insight, we can be equipped to inform them individually about sexuality. Without it, we're left with the cookie-cutter approach, the one-off uncomfortable conversation that leaves both parties with unanswered, unasked questions. This subject, and the humans involved, are too complex for that.

I have noticed that sexually well-grounded people appear to be close with others, physically, emotionally, and spiritually, like the family on the plane described in Liberators. This is not a difficult thing to do: Just let your guard down. If you have to change the way you think about relationships to make that happen, start now. Nothing inoculates against early sexual activity more effectively than parent-child connectedness, regardless of the number of parents, wealth or poverty, or race/ethnicity,[120] or even the go-to excuse, hormone levels.[121]

---

[120] Robert W. Blum and Peggy Mann Rinehart, "Reducing the Risk: Connections That Make a Difference in the Lives of Youth," (PDF

Keeping the family together matters, but simply staying married isn't the beginning and end of moral direction. Remember the guys one-upping each other in the anecdote leading off this chapter? They all came from two-parent households. So the parents' words and deeds matter. We shape the next generation's world, actively or passively.

In particular, the relationship between opposite-sex parent and child appears to frame the child's relations with opposite-sex others. This includes sexual relations, even though intercourse isn't part of parent-child relationships. I've seen this play out in my life and others', and maybe you have too: Who were the first among your adolescent peers to have sex, and what do you know of their opposite-sex parental relationships?

A daughter will see all the world's males through the lens of her experience with her father. At mating time, she will choose for or against him. Switch roles, and the same applies to the relationship between son and mother.

But it must be noted that the father's role differs from the mother's. Whereas the mother nurtures her children's development (or doesn't), the father shapes their personalities. For example, a son who grows up healthy and loved by his mother, but insecure in his masculinity, will have difficulty forming healthy relationships with both men and women. The list of potential dysfunctions from failed fathering goes on *ad infinitum*.[122]

---

download) http://tiny.cc/sexontv

[121] McIlhaney and Bush, location 197.

[122] From one tragic example cited in James Robison's *My Father's Face*, a group of prisoners was offered an opportunity to create Mother's Day cards. Their response was immediately positive. At a different time, another group was given the chance to write Father's Day cards. Few responded. http://tiny.cc/robisonbook

Further, it's probably instinctive, but parents cannot help treating sons and daughters differently.[123] Liberators will disagree, but wisdom suggests this works out for the better.

One point I learned from a child therapist is, when we parents have had the opportunity to shape our children since birth, we can't blame them when they don't act the way we hope. It makes as much sense as a potter complaining that his ball of clay turned into something ugly. But the good news is, unlike our children, we have choices in how we connect with them.

Perhaps this was organic knowledge among previous generations, who didn't have to contend with the artifices of full-time office jobs, pandering media, and the multitude of other distractions that today keep us from connecting every day with our offspring. That's up to each of us to recognize and work around.

If I had to summarize the best advice I've ever heard about childrearing in one sentence, it would be, "Treat each child the same way you will want to be treated when you're no longer able to care for yourself." That's the state in which they arrive. It may also be the state in which you depart.

Sex education lasts throughout one's early years, including images, attitudes, and words. Where parents have the advantage is being present from the start of our little ones' lives.

---

[123] Daughters display pro-social behaviors to maintain family closeness while sons focus on avoiding anti-social behaviors to avoid discipline. This is because parents report using rewards systems with daughters and punitive measures with sons. (Roche, Ahmed & Blum, 2008)

Author and speaker Mary Flo Ridley[124] aptly compares a child's mind to a sponge right out of the package. Fill it with clean water at the start, and it'll be useful for most anything. It will also repel dirty water, and rinse clean for re-use.

But if you let a brand-new sponge soak up sewage, it may never wash completely clean. There will be traces of unsavoriness at its core. This is what happens to children's minds when we allow the Liberators to get to them first.

If you recall your own development, you'll remember how difficult it was to let go of whatever you learned early. Santa Claus was just the beginning; if you were taught in grade school that humans evolved from primates, you'll have great difficulty accepting other ideas.

The Liberators know this, and they know young people tend to think in binary terms—in black-and-white. Liberators play to this by presenting all opposition as cruel, unthinking, or mentally deficient:

- You're down on free condoms in schools because you forbid others' pleasure.
- You oppose abortion because you don't know the difficulty of an unplanned pregnancy.
- You resist redefining marriage because you have a phobia.

Every conflict is presented as thinking people vs. mean, ignorant Prudes. (Nobody projects like a Liberator.) This sort of intolerance is easy to instill, and difficult to unseat.

Don't take this to imply that your own situation—or anyone's—is hopeless if you didn't get there in time to

---

[124] http://maryflo.org

prevent your children's exposure to moral corruption. Instead, let it underscore the importance of knowing what you're trying to purge, and what to replace. Maybe you didn't get the first word. You can still have the last word.

I chose the title of this book, *Sex: What Your Parents Didn't Tell You*, because I've learned what mine didn't tell me, and what yours may not have told you. It's now up to me and you to break the cycle of avoidance that delivers one generation after another to the Liberators' embrace.

Since everyone likes numbered lists, here's one that can help you keep track:

1. Open yourself to the reality of human sin, recognizing even your own sexual nature as a gift that can be used for good or bad.[125] As we discussed in What I Saw at the Buffet, humans have to eat, and humans have to mate. There's nothing inherently evil about either. It's the external overstimulation, and the internal separation of ends from means, that can divert our healthy, life-affirming drives toward destruction.

    One of the most overlooked resources for this is *Theology of the Body*[126], a series of lectures given by Pope John Paul II. Called a cultural "time bomb" for the 21st Century[127], it's an extensive read, so a

---

[125] "Good parents use the mistakes they did in the past when they were young to advise the children God gave to them to prevent them from repeating those mistakes again. However, bad parents always want to be seen as right and appear 'angelic and saintly' as if they never had horrible youth days." — Israelmore Ayivor

[126] Theology of the Body in easily accessible language at Amazon.com: http://tiny.cc/TTOBsimple

[127] Quote from George Weigel. http://tiny.cc/timebomb

more bite-sized introduction would be Christopher West's *Theology of the Body for Beginners*, or Mary Healy's *Men & Women are from Eden*. These aren't children's books, but foundational documents to help grown-ups reckon with the chaos of marriage, sexuality, and family life.

2. Be prepared to confront the popular notion that distinctions between male and female, and masculine and feminine, aren't important. We are at liberty to ignore the meaning and value of masculine traits in males, and feminine traits in females. But we are not able to change these facts any more than a ship's captain can budge a sandbar.

3. Connect every discussion of sex with its higher and greater meanings. (This is notably absent from clinical sex education.) "Why?" is the critical question in sexuality. Natural law tells us sex is a means toward two inseparable ends: procreative (1+1=3) and unitive (bonding husband and wife). "Why" can—and must, for rationality's sake—be applied to everything that surrounds sex. Without the why, sex can easily become its own end. Like the appetites we covered in What I Saw at the Buffet, this leads to self-destruction.

    For example, why is there a woman in a swimsuit on the cover of *Sports Illustrated*? Because a woman's shape captures a man's attention for the purpose of mating. The magazine salesmen hope men will buy the magazine to see more of that. Now, depending on a child's maturity level, he may or may not see the exploitation playing out here. But at least the point has been made in plain language.

4. Guard against the corrupting messages from Liberators and from the Prudes they claim to be fighting. Neither want to acknowledge that God invented sex for our benefit and wants to remain

Talking to Your Children

part of it. Liberator-concocted media narratives powerfully reinforce this point.[128]

At a young age, their entertainment must be screened. In keeping with this book's theme, it's not enough to say "No" to all that's wrong, but to say "Yes" to what's right. This means actively seeking media content that—at the very least—doesn't undermine your family's values. It takes some effort to get past the widely promoted "junk food" of pop, especially the titles we grew up with in innocence but can now see as damaging or at least not helping. (Quick: Name a Disney story that affirms the father's authority.) Like healthy food, you'll have to seek it out, and probably pay more for it, because all the widely marketed junk has economies of scale. The Internet's other side works for you in this, with an army of "mommy bloggers" passing tips and sources laterally.

Because young people have money to spend, Liberators in the entertainment industry are coming at them as hard as ever.[129] Music plants words in their head more firmly than any lecture or textbook. Pop music is carefully calculated to play on the normal longing that adolescents feel for independence, emotional comfort, identity, and beauty in life. (Do you remember wearing shirts with your favorite band's name on them? That's a grasp at identity.) So, be very careful in how you reckon with music especially. Our parents couldn't

---

[128] Never underestimate the power of narratives to influence our thinking. For example, when you come across the term "1960s," what do you picture? Probably hippies, civil-rights protests, or soldiers in Vietnam. While each had their place in that era, most Americans of the time went about their daily lives untouched by them. A more complete picture of life in the 1960s would dwarf these images.

[129] The current trend for boosting a female pop star's sales is for her to claim she's a bisexual, typically in an interview that gets explosive publicity.

have gotten between us and our bands. We can't be any more successful, nor should we try. What we can do is ask questions, innocently and genuinely, to help them engage their minds and be critical. What's your favorite song right now? Why do you like it? When the lead singer cries, "I need your love," what does that mean? You know by now that the word "love" in pop music is almost always a euphemism for sex. Help them reach that conclusion on their own.

In an age where any kid's iTouch or other wi-fi capable device can connect to the porn already whizzing around the troposphere, the best web filtering has its limits. But it's worth exploring for the home, especially in the form of accountability technology which—rather than blindly censoring content—prompts you to initiate a conversation about what they're searching for. Here again, we should put vanity aside ("I can't believe my child was looking at this!") and deal with the sin in a manner appropriate to the maturity level—our own included. If we don't accept and deal calmly with the reality that humans of all ages and social statuses choose to sin, we can't expect our children to develop a healthy sense about it.

Again, the human mind has no defense against images. For example, a pre-teen boy has no choice but to respond to the cleavage and thigh presented on the female characters in a video game. That is neither a necessary nor a naturally occurring form of sexual stimulation. Whether he understands what's happening to him is irrelevant; the bud is being forced open. Later, try to remember how tempted you were by the messages reaching you as a teen.

5. The more repressive the home life, the more appealing the Liberators' message of liberation. You may not even think you're being repressive; it's just

a reflex.

Kids eventually win. Squeezing them into a mold only raises the pressure for when they pop out. If you want to verify this, think of the most tightly repressed children you knew of in high school. Now look them up on Facebook.

Teach your own to master themselves, one habit at a time, without turning them neurotic. Sexual dysfunctions look a lot like eating disorders, and each has roots in irrational parenting practices.

6. Initiate maturity-appropriate levels of conversation. Children—adults, too—learn by connecting new information with what they already know. Start early because connections are how humans learn. Each new idea must somehow connect to one already learned. Metaphysical thought seems one of the last, valuable abilities to develop, so start with the mechanics.

   Familiarity with nature is an excellent building block for understanding sexuality. For example, when viewing a nature show together, you can talk about how animals reproduce using purely clinical language. Young children don't have the hang-ups adults have. They don't laugh about animal reproduction and they don't project human sexuality onto it. The ground is laid, then, for building toward a human and moral framework.

   Once a dialogue is ready to be established, take care not to fall back on what Ridley calls "wingy wangy words" as euphemisms for genitals. Educated people tend to use complex, cutesy, or obscure words when they're uncomfortable. Along with halting speech, it's an evasion, and children sense your discomfort and transfer it to themselves. Use medical language to get past the hangups.

7. Be the sexual role model for your child. This isn't as hard as it sounds. The culture doesn't abound with much that's positive, and since sex happens in private, you can't exactly point to a picture and say, "Like that, see?"

   The old trope about actions and words applies here. Children spot hypocrisy easily, though they don't always have the courage to point it out. If you're a married father whose eyes follow attractive women, they will notice, and your talk about monogamy won't stick. If you're a married mother who "flaunts it" in a way that draws men's attention (or fosters envy in women), think about what that's teaching your daughter.

   Once your own house is in order, you'll have a firm foundation from which to point out what's wrong with the culture around us.

8. Show them how to acknowledge temptation, so as to defuse it. This begins with simple things, like the impulse rack at the grocery store. As we approach, I announce it first: "There's the impulse items." This doesn't eliminate temptation, but it puts in plain language what's happening. Temptation can be understood, then as part of one's makeup, not an "other" thing to be split off from the personality and never properly managed. At some point, watch TV with them, with the sound off. Guess at the messages on the screen.

9. Don't delegate sex ed to the schools, church, culture, and peers. None of them have the responsibility or influence that you have, and even the most well-meaning educators get hamstrung by political rules.

   One reason I never intended this book for children is, that's your job.

10. In all things, recognize that you aren't perfect, and there will be times that you'll have to apologize, and ask forgiveness of your children. This teaches both of you about fallibility, humility, and reconciliation.

If you don't instruct your kids about sex, they will instruct you. At the least, they'll show you where you left off.

Above all, don't deceive yourself that you can shield or isolate your children. They have sexual impulses and curiosity. Cork those up, and they never learn to manage them. Many parents make this mistake with sex, and with anger. So their kids never master those drives, and essentially they carry little vials of nitroglycerine around, exploding the next time they're disturbed.

A book this size can't address all the dysfunctions to which we, as multifaceted humans, are vulnerable. (To frame this, I considered leading off this chapter with a quote from *Anna Karenina*: "Happy families are all alike; every unhappy family is unhappy in its own way." It's true, but strikes a rather cynical tone for a book emphasizing what is right about sexuality.) So, rather than try to play doctor to others—a role for which I have neither qualifications nor talent—I encourage you to believe that you can get this right for yourself and your children, and for what isn't right, to seek good advice.

In that, the people I would trust the most are priests and counselors in the Judeo-Christian traditions. They tend to see families through ups and downs over many years. Their relationships don't always have a meter running. And those who hear confessions know exactly what each of us is grappling with.

The Judeo-Christian tradition also informs our culture at every level, even though we don't often see it, like the hidden girders that shape and strengthen a skyscraper. Relationships between parent-child and husband-wife have their analogues in Scripture, which has been studied and handed along prayerfully for thousands of years.

As Dr. Lowen posited, sexuality adds up to a sum greater than "two consenting adults." It points upward, to a higher being. When we believe there's nothing there, we will inevitably turn to using—or worshipping—each other. Alternately, when we acknowledge our place in the natural order, we live life (including our sex life[130]) more fully.

If you don't presently attend a good church, find one. What's a "good" church? Start the process of elimination with the ones the Liberators have already co-opted. When their websites feature code words like inclusion, progressive, and diversity, they're not serious about morality, but about moral vanity.

I haven't church-shopped in years, but I think the obvious issue to get at is whether there's any daylight between what the church instructs on sexuality, and natural law.

A church isn't just a source of reassurance. It's supposed to be a house of healing, and of education. The secular world has six days to undo whatever you learn on the Sabbath. Spend as much time learning what's right as what's wrong. Please don't think your own level of religious schooling handicaps you in leading your family in this. It's actually a tremendous benefit to have the kids teach back to you while you all learn.

---

[130] A national survey found that churchgoers had better sex. http://tiny.cc/churchandsex

Also, see the Epilogue for additional resources.

The Prudes broke the connection between sexuality and humanity by obscuring God's role in it. To them, sex compromised their beliefs about human dignity by linking us organically to the animals through our base desires.

The Liberators preached that there is no higher purpose in life than to gratify ourselves. For them, sex is the ultimate gratification, and it has a veneer of human interaction that appears to place it above all other human acts.

If we try to knock down these messages with something that doesn't reach higher, we'll almost certainly fail. We have to supply a better narrative so that once they're making their own decisions, they can sort good information from bad.

Reaching higher in courage restores our embrace of the beauty in life and brings us one step closer to unity with God.

11
Epilogue

I wrote much of this book while sequestered in a Las Vegas hotel room.

I chose that unlikely workplace mainly because it's inexpensive and has little to do with the world I live in, and the world I want to live in, so there wasn't much of interest there to distract me.

Still, the casino floor proved irresistible for watching people. On my walk-breaks I passed rows and rows of adults feeding slot machines and tapping blackjack tables in the hope of a big payoff that would, in the end, almost certainly be denied. If questioned, many of them would say they gamble for fun, not profit. But very few appeared to be having fun. Most, in fact, looked a little like movie zombies.

I've seen a similar expression in studies of men viewing porn, and personally, on the faces of people looking for validation in dance clubs. It's a meld of fascination, want, and despair. It's how we feel when we've been promised a tantalizing, but unlikely, reward. And on those few occasions when we "win," the prize inevitably disappoints. (At least in the casino the payoff is in cash.)

The gaming industry and the Liberators have this in common: They encourage us to take risks for their reward. And once they do get our buy-in, they own us until we come to our senses again.

This is what's meant by the "slavery" of sin.

Some people live their whole lives in this kind of self-imposed bondage. In the Judeo-Christian view, that's the curse of original sin. But we can do better, when we try.

I'm grateful you've read through to the end of this book. That tells me you've learned something new and valuable, as I did in the research phase. (A phase lasting 40+ years!) I've intended this book not as an end-all, but a stepping stone. My hope is that you will continue to grow, so I've provided you with more resources below.

Please see what these authors have for you. I've referred to most of them in this book. (The quotes below aren't necessarily from the book cited beneath each quote.)

> "To a man, women seem to glow in more hues than men do, and in different ones. The spectrum is wider, the world has more music and color, just because there are women in it."

On the Meaning of Sex
J. Budziszewski, Ph.D

Professor Budziszewski has the world's second-greatest job. (The only better one I can imagine would be full-time employment as a test driver for Porsche.) Dr. Budziszewski teaches philosophy at my alma mater, The University of Texas, and writes books about natural law, sex, and related topics. His writing is often prompted by his students' questions; many of them seem even more confused by the culture than I have been, if that's possible. See also his The Line Through the Heart: *Natural Law as Fact, Theory, and Sign of Contradiction*, *Ask Me Anything: Provocative Answers for College*

Students (and its follow-up), *Written on the Heart: The Case for Natural Law*, and *How to Stay Christian in College*.

> "God made sex to be so wonderful that for a few moments, it's as if the only people who exist in the world are you and your husband. Everything is supersensitive. Your senses are heightened. You lose control."

The Good Girl's Guide to Great Sex
Sheila Wray Gregoire

Author-speaker Sheila Wray Gregoire treads where few dare: She helps women free themselves from the wrongful conviction that "good girls" aren't supposed to want and enjoy sex. Instead, she begins with the fact that God created sex as a joyful, unifying act between husband and wife, and we ought to make the most of it. Gregoire goes further to show that a woman's outward appearance of "sexiness" doesn't predict how she will fare behind closed doors—and in fact, it's often the opposite.

> "Don't be more serious than God. God invented dog farts. God designed your body's plumbing system. God designed an ostrich. If He didn't do it, He permitted a drunken angel to do it."

Summa of the Summa
Peter Kreeft

Professor Kreeft produces books faster than I can read them, and each is worthy of the time I've invested. I'm singling out *Summa of the Summa* here for its value as a stepping stone toward the mountainous *Summa Theologica*. Dr. Kreeft also wrote *A Shorter Summa* and *Summa Philosophica*, so determined is he to make St. Thomas Aquinas' foundational work accessible to all. (BTW, please don't tell Prof. Kreeft that he's way undercharging for his audio talks.)

> "The search for excitation is typical of persons who are unalive, emotionally repressed, and physically unresponsive. Lacking an inner feeling of excitement, they find life boring and empty. Sex, like any other strong stimulant, gives them a temporary feeling of excitement or aliveness."

Love and Orgasm
Dr. Alexander Lowen

As described in the Orthosexuality chapter, the late Dr. Lowen witnessed the Sexual Revolution from aside the therapist's couch. Like Alice Miller, he studied how repressive parenting warped the personalities of his patients. Reaching further as a student of Dr. Wilhelm Reich, Lowen became an expert on how emotional pathologies show up in the body itself, distorting posture, breathing, affect, and gait through chronic muscle tension. His colleagues noted how Dr. Lowen could accurately summarize a subject's emotional issues just by observing him walk, stand, and speak. But what struck me most about Dr. Lowen's ideas was how tightly they jibe with *Theology of the Body*, a work produced in complete independence and from an entirely different knowledge base. (Actually, this shouldn't surprise anyone; priests were the original therapists.) Many of

Dr. Lowen's books are out of print, so if you see one on the used market, grab it.

> "Our default is to do what our parents did.... Perhaps the topic of sex was taboo in your family growing up. What if that were different in your family today? What would that look like?"

God's Very Good Design
Mary Flo Ridley

Mary Flo speaks frankly and lovingly to parents about their responsibility to take the lead in sex education. She knows that what children want is guidance from their parents, even if they don't know how—or are afraid—to ask for it. She brings the heart of a mother and a lifetime of keen discernment to the task of adult education and encouragement. I suggest prodding your parents' group or church to sign her up for an in-person talk.

> "The call to love as God loves is stamped right into our very bodies."

Theology of the Body for Beginners
Christopher West

As noted in the previous chapter, *Theology of the Body* has been called a "time bomb" for its little-noticed potential to break the Liberators' hold on our sexual imagination. *TOTB* itself is a tall reach for many readers, so West penned this "beginners'" book for those of us who need another rung to help us start up the ladder.

> "For almost its entire existence, television has been gradually perverted by a select group of leftist individuals who have used its power to foster social change through cultural 'messaging.'"

Primetime Propaganda: The True Hollywood Story of How the Left Took Over Your TV
Ben Shapiro

This son of a Hollywood family researched the history and motivation of the creative Liberators who have propagandized the entertainment industry. Today, he finds, they've achieved more than even Sen. Joe McCarthy's followers could have imagined: ideological domination of an entire business, a blockade against contrary ideas, and a blacklist for those daring to differ. But this is no mere rant: As an inside-outsider, Shapiro supports his case with hard data showing how and why the entertainment business succeeds despite its hostility to the values of most consumers.

> "No Protestant body accepted contraception until 1930, when the Anglican bishops, meeting at their Lambeth Conference of that year, overturned all previous Lambeth pronouncements to make a narrow exception to the historic Christian teaching, allowing married couples—for "extraordinary reasons"—to practice birth control. Five hundred years earlier, the Protestant Reformers to a man thundered against all forms of birth control in words more vehement than any pope's."

Sex au Naturel
Patrick Coffin

Epilogue

Renaissance man Patrick Coffin hosts *Catholic Answers* on EWTN, critiques films, and delivers talks on issues affecting Christians. He penned this particular book to help Roman Catholics who've strayed from church teachings on contraception, and to affirm those who have lived in accordance with the faith.

> "Genuine feelings cannot be produced, nor can they be eradicated. We can only repress them, delude ourselves, and deceive our bodies. The body sticks to the facts."

Prisoners of Childhood
Alice Miller

Similar to Dr. Lowen, the late author and therapist Alice Miller understood the damage done by a style of parenting that forces children to act like adults. Her recurring theme is a child's defense mechanism of "splitting off" prohibited, strong emotions such as anger. In my reading of her works, I can understand how prudish parents especially find it tempting to withhold love in order to enforce "adult" behavior. Unfortunately, their kids never learn to integrate anger, the sex drive, longing, etc. into their personalities—the expressions Freud identified as vital. When tested by life, they veer toward explosive/muted tempers, promiscuity/frigidity, eating disorders, or drugs and drink. These pathologies aren't unique to Prude-influenced cultures, but their pervasiveness stands out once you understand the symptoms.

> "We are turning against boys and forgetting a simple truth: that the energy, competitiveness, and corporal daring of normal, decent males is responsible for much of what is right in the world."

The War Against Boys
Christina Hoff Sommers

Citing sources favorable toward masculinity is hazardous, so toxic have the media made the phrase, "men's rights." There's even an acronym, MRA, which the elites use to identify those they regard as cavemen in the area of sex and gender. It's considerably harder for them to marginalize women writing on those same issues, in particular a thorough researcher like Christina Hoff Sommers, whose *The War Against Boys* uncovers the forces in academia, government, and education working to nip masculinity in its bud. The cry, "Double standards!" used to mean something; Sommers' writings show that holding both sexes to the same standard usually means emasculating males—a price that neither male nor female can afford.

> "Engaging in sex creates a chain reaction of brain activities that lead to the desire for more sex and greater levels of attachment between two people.... The individual who goes from sex partner to sex partner is causing his or her brain to mold and gel so that it eventually begins accepting that sexual pattern as normal. For most people this brain pattern seems to interfere with the development of the neurological circuits necessary for the long-term relationships that for most people result in stable marriages and family development."

Hooked
Dr. Joe McIlhaney and Dr. Freda McKissic Bush

Cited here in several places, this book affirms scientifically what we've always known (but many deny) about ourselves: We are hard-wired to mate once and for life. Drs. McIlhaney and Bush cite volumes of studies and research in support of the principle that "sex cannot be dismissed as an activity with little or no impact on the person as a whole." The salient point is that there's no such thing as an emotional condom: Hooking up now damages one's ability to connect permanently later.

I'm closing this section, and the book itself, with an excerpt from Dr. Lowen's work that I found potentially encouraging to Prudes, Liberators, and everyone in between. No matter what we have heard, and no matter how badly we've been treated in life, there is promise for each of us through natural law:

> Reich, in *The Function of the Orgasm*, proposed a morality based upon the concept of genital self-regulation. This concept developed out of his

observation that when patients gained the capacity for full genital surrender, the whole personality of the patient changed radically. Compulsive attitudes toward work and sex disappeared. Sexual promiscuity ended, not because of any moral compulsion, but because such behavior failed to yield the satisfaction that the patient wanted. The "genital character," as Reich described the individual who had attained this capacity, had the ability to combine sex with love or love with sex: "It was as if the moral agencies disappeared completely and were replaced by better and more tenable safeguards against anti-sociality, safeguards which were not at variance with natural needs, but were, on the contrary, based on the principle that life is to be enjoyed."[131]

---

[131] Lowen, p. 314